Privilege-Resistant Policies in the Middle East and North Africa

MENA DEVELOPMENT REPORT

Privilege-Resistant Policies in the Middle East and North Africa

Measurement and Operational Implications

Syed Akhtar Mahmood
Meriem Ait Ali Slimane

WORLD BANK GROUP

1818 H Street NW, Washington, DC 20433
Telephone: 202-473-1000; Internet: www.worldbank.org

1 2 3 4 21 20 19 18

ISBN (print): 978-1-4648-1207-1
ISBN (electronic): 978-1-4648-1208-8
DOI: 10.1596/978-1-4648-1207-1

Library of Congress Cataloging-in-Publication Data has been requested.

MENA Development Report Series

This series features major development reports from the Middle East and North Africa region of the World Bank, based on new research and thoroughly peer-reviewed analysis. Each report aims to enrich the debate on the main development challenges and opportunities the region faces as it strives to meet the evolving needs of its people.

Titles in the MENA Development Report Series

Privilege-Resistant Policies in the Middle East and North Africa: Measurement and Operational Implications (2018) by Syed Akhtar Mahmood and Meriem Ait Ali Slimane

Eruptions of Popular Anger: The Economics of the Arab Spring and Its Aftermath (2018) by Elena Ianchovichina

Beyond Scarcity: Water Security in the Middle East and North Africa (2018) by World Bank

Jobs or Privileges: Unleashing the Employment Potential of the Middle East and North Africa (2015) by Marc Schiffbauer, Abdoulaye Sy, Sahar Hussain, Hania Sahnoun, and Philip Keefer

The Road Traveled: Dubai's Journey towards Improving Private Education: A World Bank Review (2014) by Simon Thacker and Ernesto Cuadra

Inclusion and Resilience: The Way Forward for Social Safety Nets in the Middle East and North Africa (2013) by Joana Silva, Victoria Levin, and Matteo Morgandi

Opening Doors: Gender Equality and Development in the Middle East and North Africa (2013) by World Bank

From Political to Economic Awakening in the Arab World: The Path of Economic Integration (2013) by Jean-Pierre Chauffour

Adaptation to a Changing Climate in the Arab Countries: A Case for Adaptation Governance and Leadership in Building Climate Resilience (2012) by Dorte Verner

Renewable Energy Desalination: An Emerging Solution to Close the Water Gap in the Middle East and North Africa (2012) by World Bank

Poor Places, Thriving People: How the Middle East and North Africa Can Rise Above Spatial Disparities (2011) by World Bank

Financial Access and Stability: A Road Map for the Middle East and North Africa (2011) by Roberto R. Rocha, Zsofia Arvai, and Subika Farazi

From Privilege to Competition: Unlocking Private-Led Growth in the Middle East and North Africa (2009) by World Bank

The Road Not Traveled: Education Reform in the Middle East and North Africa (2008) by World Bank

Making the Most of Scarcity: Accountability for Better Water Management Results in the Middle East and North Africa (2007) by World Bank

Gender and Development in the Middle East and North Africa: Women in the Public Sphere (2004) by World Bank

Unlocking the Employment Potential in the Middle East and North Africa: Toward a New Social Contract (2004) by World Bank

Better Governance for Development in the Middle East and North Africa: Enhancing Inclusiveness and Accountability (2003) by World Bank

Trade, Investment, and Development in the Middle East and North Africa: Engaging with the World (2003) by World Bank

All books in the MENA Development Report series are available for free at https://openknowledge.worldbank.org/handle/10986/2168.

Contents

Boxes

Figures

Tables

Acknowledgments

This report was prepared by a team led by Syed Akhtar Mahmood and Meriem Ait Ali Slimane and includes Edouard Al-Dahdah, Georgiana Pop, Heba Mahmoud Mokhtar Shamseldin, Francesca Recanatini, and Stephanie Trapnell. Najy Benhassine, for the Finance Competitiveness and Innovation Global Practice, provided overall guidance to the team; as did Renaud Seligmann, for the Governance Global Practice.

The following individuals contributed to various sections of this report: Georgiana Pop ("Competition Policy"), Heba Shamseldin ("Access to Finance"), Francesca Recanatini and Stephanie Trapnell ("Conflict of Interest," "Asset Disclosure," and "Freedom of Information"), and Edouard Al-Dahdah (inputs to chapter 1).

The team thanks the following colleagues for data verification and for their contribution to the design of the questionnaires that led to the data collection and the construction of the country dashboards: Martha Martinez Licetti, Melissa Johns, Gael Raballand, Mariem Malouche, Laurent Gonnet, Paul Prettitore, Peter Mousley, Gokhan Akinci, Sepehr Fotovat, Federica Saliola, Tania Ghossein, Graciela Mirales and Iulia Cojocaru, Edouard Al Dahdah. Ivan Nimac, Harald Jadlika, Yassin Sabha, Concalo Coelho, Baria Daye, and Philippe de Meneval.

The team also thanks colleagues who helped with in country data collection: Abeer Shalan, Carole Khouzami, Stefanie Ridenour, Joey Ghaleb, Nawal Filali, Zenaida Hernandez Uriz, and Julia Barrera.

The team gives special thanks to the peer reviewers who provided guidance at different stages of this report: Ishac Diwan, Joel Hellman, Melissa Johns, Stuti Khemani, Peter Ladegaard, and Renauld Seligmann.

The team extends special thanks to Patricia McCall and the INSEAD Center for Economic Growth for their support.

About the Authors

Syed Akhtar Mahmood is a lead private sector specialist in the Macroeconomics, Trade, and Investment Global Practice of the World Bank. He was Global Lead for Business Regulations and now leads the Good Regulatory Practices program at the World Bank, focusing on regulatory accountability and transparency. In his 26-year career at the World Bank, he has worked on privatization and state-owned enterprise reforms in the former socialist economies of Eastern Europe and Central Asia and Africa, as well as on private sector development issues in various regions of the world. In addition to the technical areas of trade, competitiveness, and investment climate, he is interested in the mechanics of policy reforms, including political economy, institutional and incentive issues in government, and stakeholder engagement. He earned his D.Phil. in economics from the University of Oxford in 1989. He authored a book (with Gustav Ranis) called *The Political Economy of Development Policy Change* (Blackwell, 1991), a comparative study of East Asia and Latin America.

Meriem Ait Ali Slimane is a senior private sector specialist in the Finance, Competitiveness, and Innovation Global Practice of the World Bank. She manages technical assistance and lending projects in the areas of competitiveness, value chains development, export development, e-commerce, women entrepreneurship, and business environment reforms in the Middle East and North Africa. Meriem has worked at the World Bank for seven years. She has also worked at the United Nations on green growth in Africa and in the private sector on strategy and innovation issues. She has also taught economics at the Institute of Political Sciences in Paris. Meriem is a graduate of Harvard Kennedy School, Ecole Centrale de Paris, and Ecole National Polytechnique in Algeria.

Executive Summary

Renewing the social contract—one of the pillars of the new World Bank strategy for the Middle East and North Africa (MENA)—requires a new development model built on greater trust; openness, transparency, inclusiveness, and accountable service delivery; and a stronger private sector that can create jobs and opportunities for youth in the region. Unemployment rates in the region are among the highest in the world, especially for young graduates. Recent analytic work trying to explain weak job creation and insufficient private sector dynamism points to formal and informal barriers to entry and competition. These barriers privilege a few (often unproductive) incumbents who enjoy a competition edge because of their connections or ability to influence policy making and delivery.

Policy recommendations in the field of governance for private sector policy making have been rather general and often removed from concrete, actionable policy outcomes. This book proposes to move beyond analytically documenting these issues and—for the first time—fill this policy and operational gap by answering the following question: What good governance features should be instilled in the design of economic policies and institutions to help shield them from capture, discretion, and arbitrary implementation? The objectives of this book are twofold:

- Move the debate and rhetoric on privilege, capture, and cronyism toward a more tractable and operational frame that focuses on concrete and specific policy design features that could limit opportunities for capture.
- Focus on the systemic measurement of the dimensions of policy making that could lead to discretionary and unfair behavior by (a) applying the motto of "what gets measured gets done" to the private sector governance realm and (b) offering a menu of policy entry points for policy makers to start addressing the capture issue.

The book proposes an innovative conceptual framework that encapsulates the governance features that could shield policies from capture, discretion, and arbitrary enforcement that limit competition. On the basis of this framework, a checklist of policy features in a wide range of policy areas relevant to private sector development policy is proposed, notably in terms of (a) the process of policy making (ex ante); (b) the policies and regulations and their implementation (for example, business regulations, procurement, financing, and trade); and (c) competition policies and other attributes, such as open business and transparency measures, that help identify and prevent or deter anticompetitive market behavior and outcomes (ex post).

The book benchmarks eight countries along the proposed framework and checklist of indicators, pointing, for each country, to policy gaps and poor governance features that make these countries prone to capture and discretion. The book offers operational and technical entry points to engage the capture and privilege agenda in a concrete way, which may be more politically tractable in some of our client countries.

This book also offers several tools and entry points to operationalize the *World Development Report: Governance and the Law* (World Bank 2017). In doing so, it puts an emphasis on instituting desirable functions, not insisting on mimicking good practice forms that may have worked well elsewhere. It acknowledges that progress toward less privilege and more fairness is an adaptative process for which each country should find its own entry points and sequencing to level the playing field for the private sector (Andrews, Pritchett, and Woolcock 2017).

References

Andrews, Matt, Lant Pritchett, and Michael Woolcock. 2017. *Building State Capability: Evidence, Analysis, Action.* Oxford, U.K.: Oxford University Press.

World Bank. 2017. *World Development Report: Governance and the Law.* Washington, DC: World Bank.

CHAPTER 1

Scope and Motivation of the Report

Motivation

Evidence Base

Renewing the social contract—one of the pillars of the new World Bank strategy for the Middle East and North Africa (MENA)—requires generating a new development model that is built on greater trust; openness, transparency, inclusiveness, and accountable service delivery; and a stronger private sector that can create jobs and opportunities for MENA's youth.

Unemployment rates in the MENA region are among the highest in the world, especially for young graduates (ranging between 15 percent and 25 percent). Recent analytic work trying to explain weak job creation and insufficient private sector dynamism in the MENA region all point to various formal and informal barriers to entry and competition.[1] These barriers privilege a few (often unproductive) incumbents who enjoy a competition edge because of their connections or ability to influence policy making and delivery.[2]

A number of recent studies have explicitly addressed the issue of state-business relationships in the region. In particular, detailed empirical studies on private sector policy capture for the Arab Republic of Egypt and Tunisia have exploited rich databases on politically connected firms (Diwan, Keefer, and Schiffbauer 2013; Rijkers, Freund, and Nucifora 2014). These studies have demonstrated that economic policies can be undermined in various ways to privilege a few and that this has adverse effects at both the economy and sector levels, in terms of less firm entry, higher market concentration, and slow growth performance.

World Bank (2009) provides rich evidence on how a few politically connected firms in MENA countries, by capturing the processes of policy formulation and implementation, acquire rents and privileged access to resources, and tilt the playing field in their favor. The report argues that "the success of private sector development policies rests in great part on more effective, predictable, and equitable implementation of these policies by the relevant public agencies" (World Bank 2009, xviii). It also argues for building capacity in the private sector to contribute constructively to policy debate and play an active role in the entire policy cycle from identifying to evaluating reforms.

A subsequent report, World Bank (2014a), takes the analysis further by marshaling a rich set of data (such as firm census databases for several MENA countries) and demonstrating how policy capture, by creating privileged access to resources, limited competition, and an uneven playing field, adversely affects productivity and job creation.[3] The main findings and conclusions of the report are summarized in box 1.1.

BOX 1.1

The Effects of Policy Capture

Policy capture, firm dynamics, productivity growth, and job creation in the MENA region are the key findings of *Jobs or Privileges: Unleashing the Employment Potential of the Middle East and North Africa* (World Bank 2015b).

Over the past two decades, MENA has experienced modest per capita gross domestic product (GDP) growth with low productivity growth. The structure of the economy has changed with a decline in the labor share in agriculture. However, aggregate productivity growth is mostly driven by productivity growth in sectors. MENA countries have not been able to absorb their fast-growing labor force into the higher productivity activities. Unemployment and underemployment remain high, and most workers are employed in small-scale and low-productivity activities.

So why is job creation low, both in numbers and in quality? The relationship between firm characteristics and job creation is no different in the MENA region than in others. As elsewhere, younger firms and more productive firms grow faster and create more jobs in MENA. For example, in Tunisia, 92 percent of net job creation (during 1996–2010) was in firms less than five years old and with fewer than five employees; in Lebanon, it was 177 percent between 2005 and 2010. A dynamic economy, where firm entry and exit is high, would thus contribute to productivity. However, in MENA, firm turnover has been low. Slow within-firm productivity growth and misallocation of labor and capital across firms together explain the low productivity growth in MENA.

These phenomena—low rates of firm turnover, productivity growth, and job creation—are, in turn, the result of policies that constrain competition. This is demonstrated by four case studies presented in the report. For example, a case study of foreign

(continued on next page)

BOX 1.1

The Effects of Policy Capture ***Continued***

direct investment in Jordan shows that domestic manufacturing firms (suppliers) do not benefit from foreign direct investment (FDI) spillovers, and suggest that a more liberal entry regime for foreign direct investment in Jordan's service sector will generate employment growth among domestic firms. Another case study finds "policy uncertainty" being perceived by firms as a "severe" or "major" obstacle to growth. Firms attribute much of this to discretionary practices that generate uncertainty in policy implementation. The study finds a negative effect of such discriminatory policy implementation on productivity growth and private sector dynamism (specifically the entry of new firms) in MENA.

Past industrial policies in MENA were captured by well-connected businesses and neither rewarded firms on the basis of performance nor safeguarded or promoted competition. The policy environment created privileges rather than a level playing field. These privileges insulated firms from domestic and international competition and subsidized their operations through preferential and sometimes exclusive access to cheap inputs (electricity, land, and so forth).

Using the theoretical framework proposed by Aghion et al. (2001), the study argues that such policies create artificially low costs for a small number of firms and thus generate a larger than normal cost gap between them and other firms. Such large cost gaps have reduced the incentive to be more productive for all firms. The lowest cost firms have such a large cost advantage that they do not fear catch up from others. The others are so far behind and, moreover, have the "policy card deck" stacked so much against them that they also see little hope of catching up and diverting market share to them. Because the "low-cost firms" have low productivity and no incentive to improve, and some of the others who have the capacity to become more productive have no incentive to do so, aggregate productivity has stagnated.

Conceptual Base

The *World Development Report 2017: Governance and the Law* (World Bank 2017) provides a powerful framework to understand governance malfunctions such as discretion, capture, collusion, and privileged treatment. It defines governance as the process by which state and nonstate actors design and implement policies. The setting through which different groups and actors interact and bargain over the design and implementation of policies is the policy arena. It is the setting in which governance manifests itself.

World Bank (2017) identifies the distribution of power as a main determinant of how the policy arena functions. During policy bargaining processes for the selection and implementation of policies, the unequal distribution of power—power asymmetry—can negatively affect policy effectiveness. Powerful individuals or groups who believe the outcome of certain policies risk decreasing their current or future power can use their power to block or distort the adoption of these prodevelopment policies, or undermining their implementation. The negative consequences of power asymmetries are reflected in capture, clientelism, and exclusion.

Exclusion occurs when individuals or groups are systematically sidelined from policy decisions that affect their interests. Individuals and groups with less relative power, such as small and medium enterprises, often have more difficulties bargaining for their interests and policy preferences than more powerful large firms. Exclusion then has concrete implications for inclusive economic growth.

Capture happens when powerful groups can influence policies and make them serve their narrow interests. For example, powerful and well-connected firms that operate in less-productive sectors of the economy may advocate for policies to protect their economic power, obtain preferential treatment, and block competition—with a toll on resource allocation, innovation, and productivity.

Clientelism is a third manifestation of power asymmetries; it occurs when goods and services are exchanged in return for political support. One type of clientelism takes place when public officials exchange votes from citizens in exchange for short-term benefits—such as transfers or subsidies. Accountability becomes up for sale. A second type of clientelism takes place when politicians become responsive to those groups that wield greater influence—for example, favoring the interests of telecom providers over consumers. In exchange for their political support, service providers may extract rents through the diversion of public resources, or engage in other corrupt practices, undermining equity.

World Bank (2017) shows that power asymmetries are the underlying reason why bad policies persist and good policies are not chosen or (if and when adopted) are not implemented evenly and effectively, and sometimes not at all. It demonstrates that policy effectiveness ultimately depends not only on what policies are chosen but also on how they are chosen and implemented.

In private sector development, power asymmetries leading to capture, clientelism, and exclusion manifest themselves in multiple forms:

- Explicit or informal regulatory barriers to entry in some sectors that protects incumbents or discretionary allocation of permits and licenses to connected investors to benefit a few and limit competition.
- Complex regulatory environment and discretionary enforcement of regulations that privileges nonproductive skills such as "connections to government officials."

- Government interventions of all sorts (sector policies, land policies, finance policies, incentives and subsidies, and trade barriers) that are distorted or captured to benefit a privileged few.

- Regulatory compliance enforcement that is used by (captured by) government agencies to protect dominant incumbents (for example, tax audits, inspections of all sorts—labor, municipal).

- Weak competition framework and weak enforcement capacity that limits the ability of governments to identify noncompetitive behavior and dismantle monopolistic positions.

However, power asymmetry is not the only reason for such policy ineffectiveness. A myriad of technical and capacity weaknesses make a policy system vulnerable to capture, clientelism, and exclusion, leading to discretion, arbitrariness, and privileges for the few.

The discussion of privileges may be related to the concepts of deals that Hallward-Driemeier, Khun-Jush, and Pritchett (2015) have written about, and a typology of privileges may be considered somewhat similar to the typology of deals that these authors introduced. They make three important distinctions in their paper: (a) between rules and deals, or policies and policy actions, with the former being the policy on paper (de jure) and the latter being the de facto implementation by front-line officials that can be influenced through deals; (b) between closed deals that benefit a few and open deals that benefit many; and (c) between ordered deals in which the outcomes of the deals are predictable, and disordered deals when not.

Our definition of privileges may be related to the Hallward-Driemeier, Khun-Jush, and Pritchett typology. We define privileges at two levels, that is, the ability of a few politically connected actors to influence de jure policies (rules) and de facto policy actions (closed-ordered deals). This may be termed "top-level cronyism." Open-ordered deals, accessible to many nonconnected firms, are not considered as privilege in our framework; instead they reflect systematic favoritism, albeit to many. Open-disordered deals are also not considered as privileges; they are available to many players but are somewhat unpredictable and episodic, often associated with petty corruption.

Access to privileges may not always be certain for well-connected firms. Even without any significant political change, such as regime change, there may be situations in which privileged firms cannot take their privileges for granted, and there remains a risk that these privileges may be later taken away. Alternatively, access to privileges in one area, such as government land, may not guarantee privileges in other areas, such as customs administration. We may thus think of two dimensions of the "predictability of privilege": (a) across time and (b) across policy areas. The most privileged are those who enjoy high predictability on both dimensions. The (relatively) worst are those whose predictability is low on both fronts.

Objectives and Scope of the Work

Addressing capture requires a good understanding of why and how it emerges and what opportunities exist to minimize its effect in a political economy context. A frequent critique of applying a political economy lens to development in general, and private sector led growth in particular, is its defeatism—the "go home and cry" scenario.

The focus of political economy analysis on institutions, the incentives they generate, and the effects these incentives have on development outcomes imply that reformers who want to move from "bad" to "good" equilibriums face an especially difficult, if not impossible, task. They would need to reverse the path: changing outcomes means changing incentives, which in turn means changing institutions or even creating new ones. Institutions, however, cannot be changed or created overnight—they are "sticky."

This is especially the case when the fundamental institutions—when based on authoritarianism or an oligarchy—reflect highly unequal distributions of power in the society. In such situations, institutional change necessitates major shakeup of relations between the main actors of society, of underlying power configurations. This might not be feasible and not even desirable. What is possible in these cases, however, is a more granular understanding and awareness of barriers to change, even if at the end, little can be done in the present configuration, while waiting—literally—for the "right time."

Indeed, certain moments in time—political economists speak of "critical junctures"—are especially promising for lasting change. These openings are unique events or series of events that lead to the realignment of incentives and lift preexistent constraints on action. Many factors bring about such critical junctures: domestic and international conflict, geopolitical shifts, economic booms or crises, the discovery of new natural resources, global changes in economic conditions, major episodes of technological innovation, or changes of political regimes. These openings may create unique opportunities for reforms that could lead to higher development equilibriums.

However, in the absence of such catalytic events, and given existing power configurations and constraints to change, it is still possible to improve outcomes at the margin. Moreover, a critical mass of interventions that generate such marginal outcomes may make it easier to exploit the "critical junctures" if and when they appear. This book, therefore, focuses on these incremental changes.

A recent and growing literature points to windows of opportunity in a given political economy setting in which incremental improvements are possible with substantial cumulative effect over time. Rodrik (2014) argues that although the actions of powerful interest groups, families, and individuals may be pernicious, these are not necessarily deterministic. He makes the case that new policy approaches can lead to new outcomes, even in the absence of changes to the overarching structure of political power. In the broader political economy landscape, he argues that there are opportunities to maneuver and make changes on specific technical issues at the margin (Rodrik 2014).

An appropriate mix of political mobilization and transparency measures can bring about significant change even in a challenging political economy landscape (World Bank 2016). Levy (2014) uses case studies of successful change in a diverse set of countries to discuss how virtuous cycles of change could be triggered even in weak overall governance settings through an initial set of interventions that are feasible in a given context. He thus argues for the need to "work with the grain," with an emphasis on instituting desirable functions, not insisting on good-practice forms that may have worked well elsewhere.

The *World Development Report: Mind, Society, and Behavior* (World Bank 2015d) points to the need to understand the motivations and behavioral characteristics of different players, such as politicians and government bureaucrats, and how these affect their decisions and actions (or lack thereof). According to World Bank (2015d), which draws from a rich body of literature on behavioral economics, such an understanding helps design policy interventions and reforms that stand a chance of success even in seemingly intractable situations.

The windows of opportunity are often generated in government because of the intrinsic desire on part of the bureaucracy or political leaders to do some good even in a policy environment distorted by forces that lead to capture, clientelism, and exclusion (appendix C provides a conceptual framework to illustrate such dynamics).

This work identifies entry points for operational interventions that can reduce opportunities for discretion and unleveled playing fields in key areas of private sector policy making, in a political economy context. In doing so, it goes beyond the studies referred to in the introduction. While those provided useful empirical evidence on the existence of policy capture and its deleterious effects, they have not gone far enough in identifying the poor governance features that create scope for unfair treatment and discretion. This study addresses more directly the challenge of operationalizing the good governance agenda. It provides guidance to formulating policies and governance reforms that will address the issue of privilege-driven public policy for business. It bridges the rich analytic work of the past five years in the MENA region and operationalizes good governance work in the policy areas that affect private sector development in these countries. Although focused on the MENA region, the methods and insights derived from the study will likely have broader geographic relevance.

Policy recommendations in the field of governance for private sector policy making have been rather general and often removed from concrete, actionable policy outcomes. This work intends to fill the policy and operational gaps in the following ways:

- Move the debate and the rhetoric on privilege, capture, and cronyism toward a more tractable and operational frame, focusing on the design of policy outcomes and the quality of service delivery in the regulatory area; the quality of policy implementation; and private sector policy outcomes.
- Be more concrete, operational, and specific on the technical changes needed at the policy and institutional levels.
- Focus on the systemic measurement of the various dimensions of policy making that could lead to discretionary and unfair behavior (in short, by applying the motto of "what gets measured gets done" to the private sector governance realm).

This work (a) develops a framework that encapsulates the governance features that could shield policies from capture, discretion, and arbitrary enforcement that limits competition; (b) provides a checklist of these policy features in selected areas of private sector development policy; (c) benchmarks where MENA countries stand in each of the above areas, in terms of how much of these policy and good governance features are prevalent; and (d) offers operational guidance on how this policy agenda can be moved forward.

It is important to understand what this study does not do. It does not provide additional analytical evidence on the issues constraining private sector growth—instead, it starts with the existing evidence and focuses on the question, "what can be done?" It does not provide analytical evidence that transparency, accountability, stakeholder participation, and other attributes of good governance reduce opportunities for capture, discretion, and policy distortions that mute competition. It does not seek to provide evidence on the overarching political economy ecosystem, such as the political system or channels of influence (for example, collective action by businesses). Finally, it does not measure the levels of capture, clientelism, exclusion, discretion, arbitrariness, and corruption. Rather, as illustrated in figure 1.1, this work focuses on the policies and institutions, their design, and their implementation (symbolized by the middle rectangle in the figure) rather than the political context upstream or the measurement of the actual symptoms of policy ineffectiveness.

This report adds value by presenting a new set of indicators that enables granular assessment of the vulnerability to privilege seeking of both individual policy areas as well as the overall policy regime. The indicators are couched in concrete operational terms (for example, existence of policies, laws, systems, and practices); thus, the move from measurement to identification of actions is relatively straight forward. The indicators capture both de jure and de facto dimensions and the report brings out the need to look at both. The report discusses interactions between different policy areas that may help in identifying potential synergy between different intervention areas and the sequencing of reform actions in specific country contexts. Finally, it brings together insights from different strands of literature to provide a fairly comprehensive picture of the privilege-resistant agenda.

The benchmarking of the degree of privilege resistance (or its flip side, vulnerability to capture) may create demand for change, while the granular and operational nature of the exercise may facilitate action in response to

FIGURE 1.1

Ecosystem of Capture, Discretion, and Arbitrariness

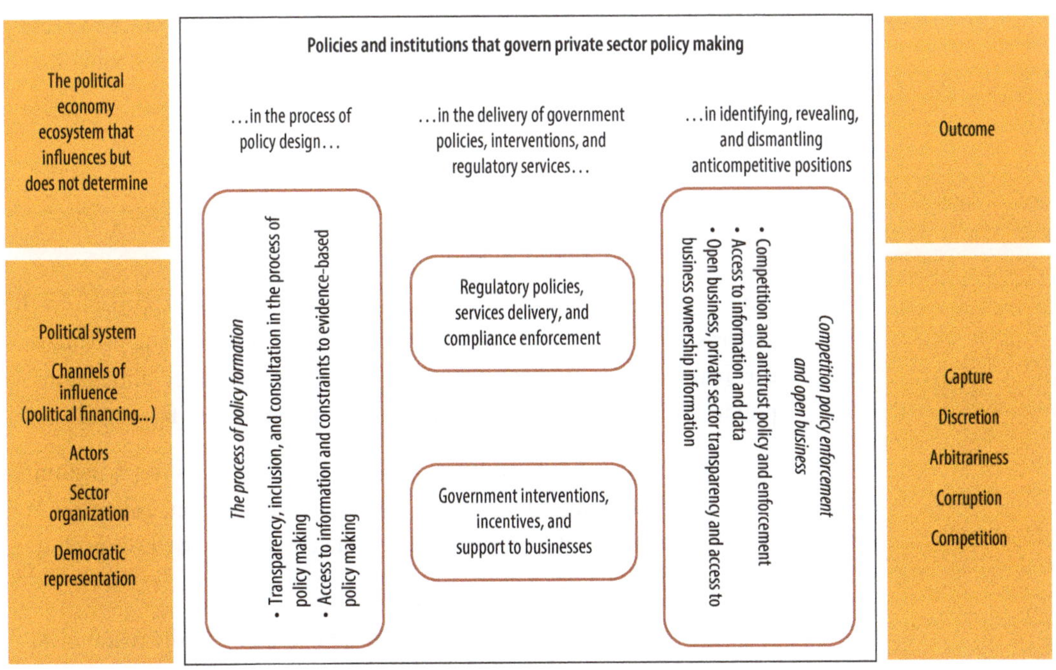

such demand. Many operational interventions implied by this report have been implemented in different countries. However, these interventions may not have been viewed through the "privilege-resistant" lens, and, thus, their potential to address privilege may not have been fully realized. By providing this lens, the report hopes to catalyze a better packaging of interventions that may make a substantial dent in privilege seeking systems.

The report will likely appeal to a wide audience. Governments will find the methodology useful for identifying vulnerabilities in their policy areas and may use it for self-assessments of the privilege resistance of policy areas. Moreover, while this report does not provide in-depth country assessments, it provides enough country-specific information for individual governments to discuss a privilege-resistant policy agenda and identify a set of initial operational interventions. In addition, governments may expand on the assessment by applying the report's methodology to collect more in-depth information on the policy areas covered, or on additional policy areas.

Nongovernmental stakeholders, including business leaders, who would like to see a move from a privilege-driven policy regime toward greater competition, may find the report's findings useful as an advocacy tool, both to raise awareness of the issue and to push for concrete operational interventions. Development partners may consult the report as they use their programs to help support privilege-resistant policy making and design specific programs and interventions. It may also help in improving coordination between donors operating in individual countries to create a critical push for the agenda. In the World Bank Group, as discussed in the final chapter, the report will help in identifying entry points for operational interventions, including opportunities for collaboration in this area across global practices and other units.

Working Analytical Framework

This report adapts the World Bank's (2017) conceptual approach to the process of policy making and policy implementation for the private sector. It proposes a working framework that captures three dimensions of policy making in the private sector area (summarized in figure 1.2):

- *Process of policy formation* (left rectangle)—including bargaining between concerned actors, for the identification, selection and adoption of policies; who is included in this process; who is excluded; and the barriers to entry to the policy arena.
- *Quality of the policies and of their implementation* (middle rectangles)—whether regulatory policies (for example, licensing, permits, sector

FIGURE 1.2

Conceptual Framework for Analyzing Discretion and Capture

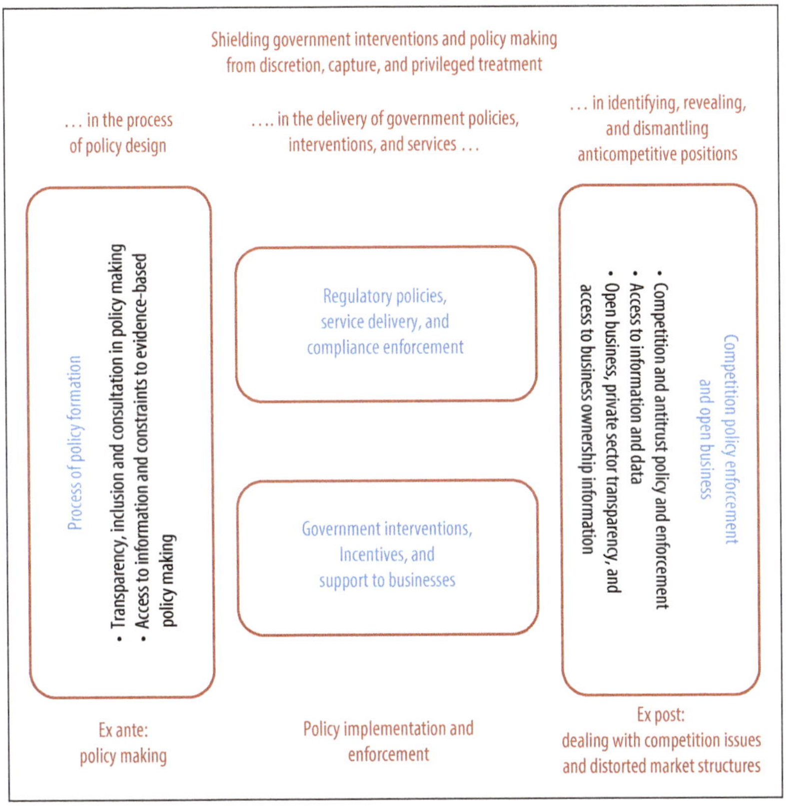

regulations, trade policy and customs), or more active policy interventions (for example, investment incentives, state-owned enterprises, access to land).

- *Set of rules that restrict anticompetitive market behavior*: these include competition policy frameworks and public accountability mechanisms; the latter restricting conflict of interest and encouraging financial disclosure and right to information, hence creating disincentives to privilege seeking and giving.

Capture, collusion, exclusion, discretionary treatment, and noncompetition in the marketplace take place in the process of policy formation (left column in figure 1.2). The effect of these forces, is most explicitly felt in individual policy areas, both in the policies and regulations as written on paper as well as in the manner they are implemented in practice (middle column in figure 1.2). These policies include both: (a) regulatory policies, service delivery and compliance; and (b) government interventions, incentives and support to businesses.

Weaknesses in the individual policy areas create noncompetitive outcomes in the marketplace. It then falls on competition policy to address these deficiencies to enhance the level of competition in various markets and curb anticompetition behavior by powerful incumbents (right column in figure 1.2). Where the competition policy framework is weak, such deficiencies remain unaddressed. This generates a vicious cycle as the persistence of a noncompetitive marketplace increases the power of rent-seeking incumbents and their ability to influence subsequent government decisions. The following sections discuss further the three columns in figure 1.2.

Process of Policy Formation

Policies, laws, and regulations affect the distribution of power and resources. They may generate new sources of rents, or eliminate existing ones. Support or opposition to such policies and regulations depend on the distribution of gains and losses and may be passive or active, depending on the power of the groups affected, the extent of their mobilization, and their willingness to spend political capital in pursuit of their interests. Such political economy dynamics often create a wedge between a technically optimum solution and the solution (policies, laws, regulations) that is adopted and implemented.

This problem is accentuated if a government does not have a tradition of evidence-based policy making. Information plays an important role. In a political economy context, lack of information or data often constrains evidence-based policy making. This creates space for interest groups to advocate policies and regulations that diverge from the technically optimum. The problem is exacerbated by poor information flows from government to businesses, which often create asymmetry of information in the business sector. Well-connected businesses may get to know about government's policy and regulatory plans in advance and prepare to advocate, while others are caught unguarded. Features of good policy formation processes include the following:

- Governments give notice of planned policy and regulatory changes, share draft policies and regulations with stakeholders through an inclusive consultative process, and consider stakeholder feedback;
- Policies and regulations are based on solid technical analysis;
- Results of such analyses are made public; and
- Policies and other reforms follow from broader strategies and are consistent with other relevant policies.

Evidence-based policy making needs to be inclusive so the evidence reflects the issues, opportunities, and constraints relevant to—and views expressed by—a broad range of businesses. Inclusivity is enhanced by better disclosure of information by governments because this allows a broad range of people to take informed decisions in their businesses and participate effectively in the policy-making process. This includes information on government contracts or other government commitments that have fiscal or revenue implications, such as tax incentives or power purchase agreements. Governments may also publicly disclose economy-wide and sector statistics, such as on tax, customs, wages, and industrial production. Information such as these often confer market power, and, thus, their widespread availability helps create a level playing field for market players. There is a continuum of disclosure scenarios ranging from limited disclosure to a small number of people to free disclosure to the public. Many types of disclosure may be considered along this continuum.

Governments are often nontransparent about their policy and regulatory intentions. New policies, laws, regulations, and standards are often announced without prior discussion with stakeholders on the rationale and content of the initiatives. Apart from creating unpredictability and lack of ownership, such initiatives often lead to low-quality outputs because they are not informed by the experience and knowledge of stakeholders. Sometimes, even in government, lower level officials charged with implementation are unaware of the changes, leading to implementation gaps.

The content of policies, laws, regulations, and standards may or may not contain provisions that promote transparent and rule-based interactions between economic actors. Even when such provisions exist on paper, their administration or enforcement may fall short or may favor some beneficiaries over others. The disclosure of the outputs of state action is key to empowering citizens to hold governments accountable. Information related to outputs—who benefits from the policies (for example, which firms receive tax incentives, land-use rights, building permits)—is vital to help citizens gauge whether state resources are being allocated fairly.

Government Policies, Interventions, and Regulatory Services

The second important dimension is the quality of the design and implementation of specific policies and other government interventions aimed at private sector development. One key factor is the prevalence of rule-based decision making and service delivery, in which any discretion follows well-defined rules. At one end of the spectrum are cases in which a government official confers a benefit such as tax incentives, or performs a regulatory function, such as issuing a construction permit, in a discretionary manner with no reference to any predetermined criteria. Businesses whose applications have been rejected do not know why. No information is shared, even in the office, on the recipients and amount of incentive granted to each. The scope for discretion is reduced, although not fully eliminated, when a predetermined set of criteria exists, even if not always followed. At another end of the spectrum are cases in which clear rules or templates for decision making are consistently followed. Disclosure of information, even if only to a limited number of people, may encourage objective rule-based decision making with any discretion disclosed to relevant parties. Features of nondiscretionary government policies, interventions, and regulatory services include the following (see also the "From Conceptual Framework to Measurement" section):

- Regulations do not prevent entry and competition and do not entail excessive discretionary decisions.
- Regulatory enforcement follows well-defined criteria (for example, selection of enterprises to be inspected is based on risk-based mechanisms; inspectors follow checklists when inspecting companies).
- Award of privileges (for example, investment incentives or industrial land) follow well-defined criteria and information on the awards is widely shared.
- There are good business-to-government feedback mechanisms on the quality of reform implementation and regulatory delivery.
- Important sectors are not subject to any policies or regulations that are onerous, costly, or time-consuming, or that frequently change, thereby creating "policy uncertainty."
- If state-owned enterprises operate in the markets, they do not receive preferential treatment not available to other firms that may limit competition.

Identifying, Revealing and Deterring Anticompetitive Behavior

Many markets in MENA countries are not fully functioning, and private sector participation is limited. This is because restrictive product market regulations and sector-specific constraints created by government policies limit entry or affect firms' capacity to compete in specific sectors; and because ineffective enforcement of competition rules allows for anticompetitive business practices. On the basis of currently available Global Competitiveness Review Indicators, five out of 12 MENA countries score in the bottom decile in terms of intensity of local competition and the effectiveness of competition (antimonopoly) policies among 148 countries. Even countries in which competition frameworks have been enacted more than 10 years ago face challenges; this is the case of Algeria, Jordan, Morocco, and Tunisia. Enhancing the competition policy framework and its enforcement is a critical agenda in the region.

As with other weaknesses in the competition policy framework that prevent the detection of anticompetitive behavior, existing rules often enable significant distortion (for example, exemptions for cartels without any well-defined criteria for such exemptions). As in the other policy areas to be studied, here too the aim of the exercise will be to identify the room for such discretion in the competition policy framework. A strong government's ability to assure competition entails an effective competition law and a functional competition authority in place; relevant questions to ask include the following:

- Can the competition authority's decisions be vetoed by line ministries or any other body of the executive branch?
- Who allocates the budget of the competition authority (for example, parliament, government, self-financing through merger filling or fines, other)?
- Is the competition authority governed by a single chairman or a collegiate body)?

In addition, there needs to be transparency in private sector operations (open private sector). One test is whether the ownership and beneficiaries of private sector operations are disclosed.

From Conceptual Framework to Measurement

The conceptual framework in this report illustrates the need for developing tools and measures for policy areas to help determine where countries stand on the dimensions of governance for private sector policy making. Various elements and features of policies, regulations, and institutions may reduce the risk of discretion, unequal treatment, and arbitrariness for private sector firms. These features will vary by specific policy area, and will likely include elements such as openness and transparent practices, accountability for results, and the design of regulations and policies that promote competition.

This work therefore focuses on analysis and the development of measurements. In terms of measures, the exercise considers the policy areas listed in table 1.1. The policy areas studied portray the principal elements of a framework to shield government regulatory and promotional policies from the effectiveness-sapping consequences of administrative discretion and capture by vested interests. The list is not comprehensive but represents important channels through which privilege is granted to businesses, or the process of privilege seeking is affected. These are the principal channels or entry points through which measurable actions can be identified and taken by policy makers to ultimately strengthen the private sector economic and job growth performance.

The stock-taking applied to each policy area consisted of two phases:

- Phase 1: Development of the framework and the diagnostic method (on selected policy areas)
- Phase 2: Collection of data in eight MENA countries—Algeria, Egypt, Jordan, Kuwait, Lebanon, Morocco, Oman, Tunisia—and four comparator countries (France, Italy, Portugal, and Spain); in addition to the qualitative data specially collected for this study, secondary quantitative data were used.

The diagnostic method developed for benchmarking countries is a critical element of this exercise. The methodology relies on questionnaires or checklists of indicators, pointing, for each country, to policy

TABLE 1.1

Policy Areas Studied

Overall process of policy formation
Regulatory policy areas
• Customs and trade policy
• Business regulation
Active policy areas
• Public procurement
• Allocation of public land
• Investment incentives
• Access to finance
Competition policy and practice
Public accountability mechanisms
• Conflict of interest restrictions
• Financial disclosure
• Freedom of information

gaps and poor governance features that make these countries prone to capture and discretion. The checklists assess where MENA countries stand in each policy area (listed in table 1.1) in terms of how much of the privilege-resistant policy governance features are prevalent or not.

In practice, the policy checklists take the form of questionnaires (available in appendix A) that ask binary questions about the existence and features of specific policies, regulations, and institutions. The questionnaires cover de jure (policies and laws on paper) and de facto (the reality of implementation) aspects. The questionnaires cover several policy areas with focus on the notions of transparency, fair opportunity, access to information accountability, and integrity. These questionnaires aim at identifying the breaches for privilege at different levels of interactions of the private sector with the government and its administration. They can identify opportunities for high-level capture, such as in the case of public procurement, access to public land, and incentives or petty privileges in the case of tax collection.

Privilege-Resistant Features in Core Policy Areas

From the point of view of privilege resistance, the critical feature of a policy area is the set of mechanisms that promote rule-based decision making (including discretion that is justified but based on rules). The centrality of this is depicted in figure 1.3, which also shows other features of policy areas covered by this study. Two sets of factors strengthen rule-based decision making by creating accountability mechanisms that reveal violations of rule-based protocols. These are grievance or redress mechanisms, and integrity mechanisms addressing fraud and corruption. Further reinforcement is provided by transparency arrangements, such as consultation with stakeholders and sharing of information with the public. All these features operate more effectively if underpinned by a strong policy, legal, and institutional framework.

The rule-based decision-making feature can be captured through appropriate questions in different policy areas. For example, other things remaining the same, the award of investment incentives may be more rule-based if the grants are based on a review or screening process by the authorities in charge of incentive administration, and if this is based on a set of criteria published in advance. Similarly, when customs declarations for imports are electronically processed, there is less likelihood of discretionary treatment. Some features may expand the space for discretionary treatment, for example, "hidden requirements" for obtaining business registration or construction permits, or no requirement for tax inspectors to explain the reasons for inspections. Table 1.2 provides examples of

FIGURE 1.3

Privilege-Resistant Policy Features

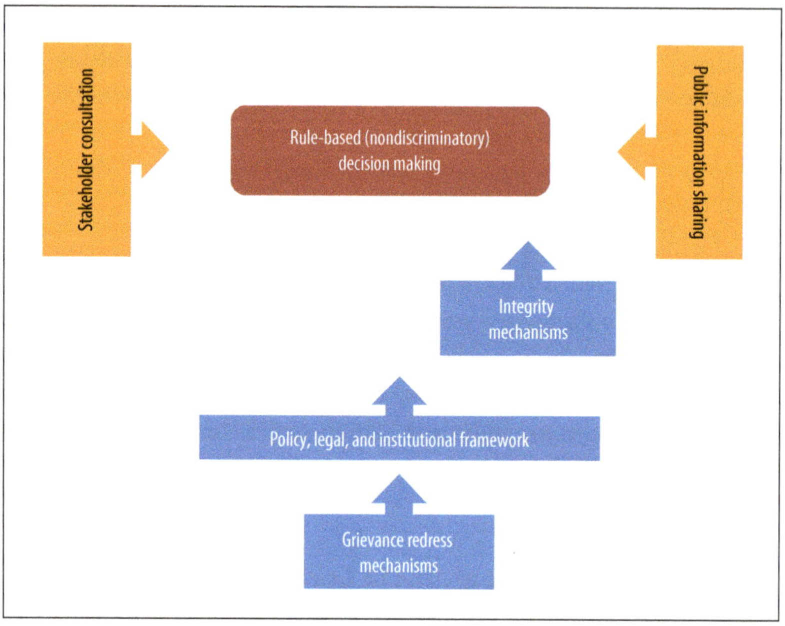

TABLE 1.2

Questions That Reflect Rule-Based Decision Making

Policy area	Examples
Customs and trade policy	Are customs declarations electronically processed for imports—at least at the main ports?
Business regulation	Are there informal requirements for obtaining business registration, in addition to the official ones?
	Are there hidden "procedures" for obtaining construction permits in addition to the official ones?
	In practice, do authorities follow risk-based approaches to planning tax inspections?
	Is the purpose of the tax inspection visit clearly stated?
Investment incentives	Are investment incentives granted based on a review or screening process by the authorities in charge of incentive administration? If so, is this based on a list of criteria published in advance?
Allocation of public land	Is public industrial land allocated to the private sector...
	• ...through auctions or tenders?
	• ...after a cost benefit or business plan analysis?
	• ...after a due diligence process?
Public procurement	By regulation:
	Do public opening of tenders follow a defined and regulated procedure?
	Are records of proceedings for bid openings are retained?
	Are records of proceedings for bid openings are available for review?
	Are security and confidentiality of bids maintained prior to bid opening?

questions used in this study to capture policy features that relate to rule-based decision making.

Grievance and redress mechanisms allow aggrieved parties to express their grievances, triggering fair and adequate responses by government, including justifications for negative decisions. However, the mere existence of a grievance mechanism is not enough. It is vital that government agencies take the mechanisms seriously and make a sincere, fair attempt to address the grievance. All grievances are not expected to be justified or possible to resolve; in such cases, good practice is for the agency to explain to the aggrieved party the reasons for not taking the expected remedial measure. Time is essential: the effectiveness of grievance mechanisms is enhanced if there are limits on how much time government agencies can take to address grievances and inform businesses about decisions. Table 1.3 contains examples of questions used in the study to capture this dimension.

Integrity mechanisms, by detecting and addressing fraudulent and corrupt behavior, increase the costs of discretionary treatment and thus strengthen incentives for rule-based decision making. For example, in the case of public procurement, if the regulatory framework covers fraud and corruption, provides a definition of each, and spells out the individual responsibilities and consequences for government employees found guilty of fraud or corruption in procurement, it may increase the likelihood of procurement decisions being based on rules rather than discretion. A number of questions were asked in different policy areas to capture such features (table 1.4).

TABLE 1.3

Questions to Reflect Mechanisms for Grievance, Complaints, and Redress

Policy area	Examples
Customs and trade policy	By regulation: • Is there a possibility to appeal decisions? • Is there an official timeframe for appeal? • Is there a possibility of recourse to independent jurisdiction in the final instance?
Business regulation	By regulation, are there appeal mechanisms regarding construction permits? In practice, are the appeal mechanisms used and effective? By regulation, are there grievance reporting and redress mechanisms regarding tax inspections? In practice, are there grievance reporting and redress mechanisms regarding tax inspections?
Investment incentives	Does the law allow the affected investor to appeal to a higher authority once a decision has been taken based on the application on incentives by the administrating authority? Does this happen in practice?
Allocation of public land	By regulation: • Does the industrial land authority provide arguments and explanations when it renders a negative decision? • Is it possible to appeal a negative land allocation decision? Is there an independent body to which applicants can appeal against the decision of the industrial land authority? By regulation, is the appeal committee required to render a decision within a specific time frame?
Public procurement	Does the regulatory framework: • Provide for the right of participants to ask for an independent review in a procurement process? • Establish timeframes for issuance of decisions by the administrative review body?

TABLE 1.4

Questions to Reflect Mechanisms for Detecting Fraudulent and Corrupt Behavior

Policy area	Examples
Customs and trade policy	Are there financial incentives for customs officials to discover fraud?
	If yes, what are the incentives for customs agents to discover fraud? No incentive; a flat incentive; a percentage of the fine?
	Is the incentive to discover fraud capped?
Public procurement	Does the regulatory framework cover fraud and corruption?
	Does the regulatory framework provide a definition of what is considered fraud and corruption?
	Does the regulatory framework spell out the individual responsibilities and consequences for government employees, and private firms or individuals, found guilty of fraud or corruption in procurement?
	Is there a secure, accessible, and confidential system for the public reporting of cases of fraud, unethical behavior, and corruption?

Incentives for rule-based decision making is strengthened by transparency measures that involve sharing of information and consultation with stakeholders. Studies in several areas have shown the power of information and transparency in influencing decisions by various actors, including government officials, and thus improving outcomes (for example, Stiglitz 2002). For example, it has been demonstrated that (a) requirements on pollution disclosure can help reduce pollution levels; (b) fiscal transparency and participatory budgeting can lead to better outcomes in terms of both allocation of public resources and the efficiency of their use; and (c) cross-country indicators of performance can trigger actions by governments in poorly performing countries (as evidenced by the reform momentum generated by the World Bank Group's Doing Business Indicators). Such evidence has triggered growing interest in the World Bank Group on governance-related benchmarking, for example, in the social sectors.[4]

Similar considerations apply to the policy areas covered by this study. Thus, other things remaining the same, customs officials are less likely to go for unduly discretionary valuation of imports if tariff data are publicly available. More generally, their scope for arbitrary behavior will be restricted if the customs code, and trade clearing procedures and formalities are also publicly available, preferably on a web site. Similarly, rule-based decision making may be encouraged in the case of business regulations if the compliance requirements, such as procedures to be followed, fees to be paid and documents to be provided, are clearly stated and made publicly available.

Another set of transparency measures relates to publication of the decision outcomes. Examples include a publicly available annual report on allocated public industrial land. This practice will be sustainable if buttressed by law, that is, if the relevant authority is required by law or regulation to publish such a report. Another example is the practice of publicly sharing information about investment incentives granted during a year. Such a practice, again buttressed by law, may increase the likelihood of such incentives being granted in a rule-based manner. Taking another example, a public procurement process may be conducted according to cost and quality-based selection rules. However, to assure that the process is fair and any discretion is aimed at achieving an efficient allocation of resources, the minutes of the decision process may be recorded, kept on file, and shared with bidding firms. In cases in which public disclosure does not threaten citizens' (or firms') privacy, it may be appropriate for the service provider to publicly disclose policy outcomes, such as identification of winning bids and firms.

Finally, transparency is enhanced when there is a practice of consulting stakeholders on important matters, such as draft laws, regulations, and rules. Here, too, a legal requirement to carry out such consultations may be important, especially in countries where such consultation traditions are weak. Information on the outcomes of the award process, including of nonawards (for example, the number of rejections and reasons), may be disclosed to key ministries in the government or key oversight bodies such as parliamentary committees. Examples of questions that capture these dimensions of transparency for various policy areas are provided in table 1.5.

Finally, strong policy, institutional, and legal frameworks help enhance resistance to privilege seeking and granting. For example, this may happen in the case of public procurement if there exists an oversight body with its own budget that is free of conflict of interest (for example, not involved in procurement operations by law and in practice), and if there is an institutionalized multiyear procurement planning exercise. In the case of public land allocation, a public industrial land allocation system and a dedicated, independent management authority may help narrow the scope for privilege seeking. In the case of investment incentives, the lack of a good policy framework increases the likelihood of discretionary award of incentives. A good incentive policy would clearly articulate the principles of the award process, and have provisions for publishing information on the incentives offered and for periodic government review of the incentive regime to assess the results and reform the regime if needed.

TABLE 1.5

Questions to Reflect Transparency

Policy area	Examples
Customs and trade policy	Are tariff data publicly available on a web portal accessible to all?
	Are trade clearing procedures and formalities publicly available on a web portal?
	Is the customs code publicly available?
Business regulation	By regulation, are the requirements for obtaining business registration specified on a web portal or at the regulator's office?
	By regulation, are the fees for obtaining construction permits publicly available on a website or national gazette?
	By regulation, are the tax compliance requirements published and accessible on a web portal or at the relevant authority?
	In practice, do the relevant agencies inform applicants about decisions or delays in providing construction permits within a specified time frame?
Investment incentives	Does the law require consultation at the time of formulation of the relevant laws, regulations, and decrees relating to incentives?
	De facto, is an interested or affected investor given an opportunity to comment on the relevant laws, regulations, and decrees relating to incentives before their finalization?
	Does the government maintain a central database or inventory of investment incentives that provides a comprehensive list of incentives being offered to investors? If so, is the inventory published in a publicly available source?
	Does the government publicly share information about incentives awarded in the past, including budgeted and awarded funds per year, as well as the number of beneficiaries?
Allocation of public land	Is the land authority required by law or regulation to publish a report of allocated public industrial land every year?
	De facto, does the land authority publish a report of allocated public industrial land every year?
	Is this report available to the public either on a web portal or in a national gazette?
Public procurement	Is there an integrated information system that provides, at a minimum, up-to-date procurement information, including contract award information?
	Is this information system accessible to the public at no or minimum cost?

Several questions reflecting such features were included for various policy areas to capture the presence of such policy, institutional, and legal frameworks.

New Measurement Tool: Country Dashboards

The features of the foundational areas—policy formation process, competition policy, and public accountability mechanisms—are explained and discussed in detail in chapter 2 and cover eight countries in the MENA region: Algeria, Egypt, Jordan, Lebanon, Kuwait, Morocco, Oman, and Tunisia. For some policy areas, these countries have been benchmarked against European comparators: France, Italy, Portugal, and Spain.

Our systematic country assessments in different policy areas have generated synthetic country dashboards that may be viewed as quick diagnostic tools (figure 1.4). These help identify subpolicy areas that have left space for privilege, discretion, and arbitrariness and need to be reformed to level the playing field for the private sector. For each country, the policy areas are graded as to their degree of vulnerability to privilege seeking.

The data underlying these dashboards were collected between May and July 2015 through topic experts' interviews in each country. Topic experts (inside and outside the World Bank Group) were mobilized in the following policy areas: trade and customs, public procurement, access to public industrial land, access to finance, business regulation, and incentives policy. Data on North African countries were collected by the competition team of the World Bank, and remaining countries' data were collected through experts' interviews. Data on public accountability mechanisms were collected by the Governance Global Practice of the World Bank for half the countries and completed by experts' interviews for the other countries. Citizen engagement data were sourced from the World Bank's Global Indicators of Regulatory Governance in 2016.

The data do not result from firm or government officials' surveys and do not reflect respondents' perceptions. The treatment of data is not statistic as it would be the case for survey data, and the questionnaires included binary questions that led to scores of zero for a negative feature and 1 for a positive feature (for example, either the law or agency in question exists or not; either there is a publicly available database or not). Furthermore, collected data went through a round of verifications by World Bank staff knowledgeable about the countries and policy areas.

For each policy area, the composite score is the average of the binary scores obtained for all questions. The composite score determines the degree of resistance to privilege in the policy area and in the country in question. Four intervals follow the rules described hereafter. This arbitrary segmentation is a first try to rank the countries according to the resistance of their policies to privilege, discretion, and arbitrariness. Another way of segmenting the countries would have been to rank them according to their distance to the average (above or below) or their distance to the frontier (the best performer). One extreme option would have been to use the O-ring theory and consider that a negative answer for a key feature of one subpolicy area would annihilate the entire subpolicy area (for example, the absence of a central bank's regulation regarding lending to related parties would annihilate the entire section on lending to related parties in the finance policy area and reduce that score to zero).

FIGURE 1.4

Dashboards of Privilege Resistance for Eight MENA Countries, 2015

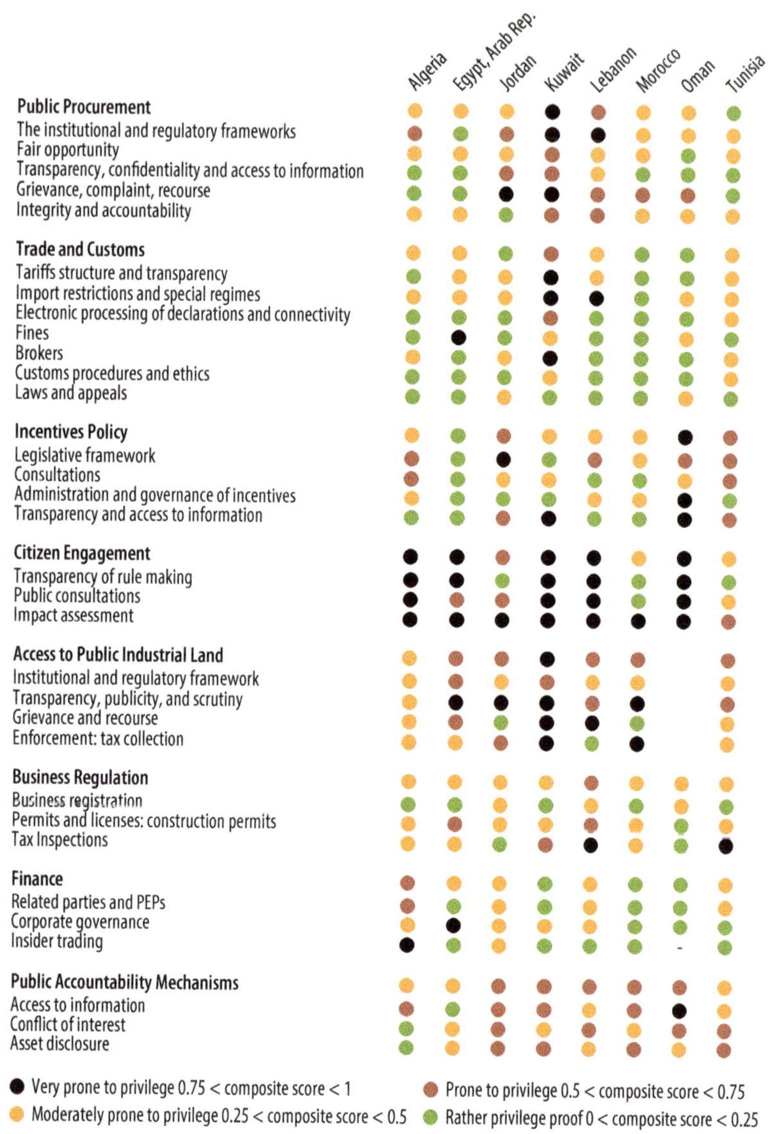

Source: World Bank.
Note: PEP = politically exposed person.

Caveats and Limitations

The database used for the country dashboards consists of indicator values for different dimensions of the policy areas studied for the eight MENA countries and four European comparator countries. These values are essentially binary numbers, which indicate whether certain features (for example, institutions, policies, practices) exist for these policy dimensions. The values are based mostly on the knowledge, and sometimes on the judgements, of experts familiar with the respective policy areas in the countries. The experts were also provided with detailed guidance on how to carry out their assessments. Nonetheless, binary scoring has its limitations. Some degree of subjectivity creeps into the assessments and often there are gray areas that cannot be adequately captured by such scoring. Therefore, the data in the following dashboards are only indicative as they result from a first data collection exercise and can be improved through subsequent data collection rounds.

The obtained dashboards might provide a rosier picture of countries' privilege resistance. The data reflect only the policy areas that are covered through the questions asked. Other sets of questions would have led to other results. In this first attempt to diagnose and assess the privilege resistance of countries, the questionnaires or checklists aimed at covering the essential breaches through which discretion, arbitrariness and therefore privilege and preferential treatment could occur. Another limitation of this data collection exercise is the fact that the questionnaires are a blend of de facto and de jure questions, sometimes assessing policies on paper and sometimes their implementation. The questionnaires might be skewed toward the de jure aspect of policies—that is, laws and regulations, on paper—more than the de facto aspect, that is, the reality of their implantation on the ground and how. This could provide a rosier picture of the reality of privilege-resistant policies. For example, in chapter 2, we will see that the de jure situation in terms of incentives is often better than the de facto one.

One area of improvement of the diagnostic exercise is to separate these two aspects and assess more deeply the extent to which policies are well, or fully, implemented on the ground and what are the flaws and gaps to draft precise recommendations. A deeper look into each country through another round of analysis could go further into the de facto situation. Deep dives in several MENA countries will be conducted later to deepen the understanding of privilege issues in each context.

Notes

1. These include Rijkers, Freund, and Nucifora (2014); Schiffbauer, Diwan, and Keefer (2013); World Bank (2009, 2014a, 2014b, 2015b). Also closely related is World Bank (2014c).
2. Appendix B summarizes the findings and recommendations of these studies.
3. The analysis combines these data sources with two novel data sets that identify the first-tier politically connected firms in the Mubarak and Ben Ali regimes in Egypt and Tunisia, respectively.
4. It is important not to overstress the power of transparency. It has been argued in the literature that it is not transparency per se but the confluence of transparency and political engagement that often brings about change.

References

Diwan, Ishac, Philip Keefer, and Marc Schiffbauer. 2013. *The Effect of Cronyism on Private Sector Growth in Egypt*. Washington, DC: World Bank.

Hallward-Driemeier, Mary, Gita Khun-Jush, and Lant Pritchett. 2015. "Deals versus Rules: Policy Implementation Uncertainty and Why Firms Hate It." Policy Research Working Paper 5321, World Bank, Washington, DC.

Philippe Aghion, Christopher Harris, Peter Howitt, and John Vickers. 2001. "Competition, Imitation and Growth with Step-by-Step Innovation." *Review of Economic Studies* 68 (3): 467–92.

Rijkers, Bob, Caroline Freund, and Antonio Nucifora. 2014. "All in the Family: State Capture in Tunisia." Policy Research Working Paper 6810, World Bank, Washington, DC.

Rodrik, Dani. 2014. "When Ideas Trump Interests: Preferences, Worldviews, and Policy Innovations." *Journal of Economic Perspectives* 28 (1): 189–208.

Stiglitz, Joseph. 2002. "Transparency in Government." In *The Right to Tell: The Role of Mass Media in Economic Development*, edited by Roumeen Islam, 27–44. WBI Development Studies. Washington, DC: World Bank.

World Bank. 2009. *From Privilege to Competition: Unlocking Private-Led Growth in the Middle East and North Africa*. Washington, DC: World Bank.

———. 2014a. *Jobs for Shared Prosperity: Time for Action in the Middle East and North Africa*. Washington, DC: World Bank.

———. 2014b. "More Jobs, Better Jobs: A Priority for Egypt." World Bank, Washington, DC.

———. 2014c. "Why Doesn't MENA Export More? A Firm-Level Perspective." Unpublished report, World Bank, Washington, DC.

———. 2015a. *Enabling Implementation of Public Procurement Reform in MENA Countries: A Case Study of Jordan and Morocco*. Washington, DC: World Bank.

———. 2015b. *Jobs or Privileges: Unleashing the Employment Potential of the Middle East and North Africa*. Washington, DC: World Bank.

———. 2015c. *Tunisia: Systematic Country Diagnostic*. Washington, DC: World Bank.

———. 2015d. *World Development Report 2015: Mind, Society, and Behavior*. Washington, DC: World Bank.
———. 2016. "Making Politics Work for Development: Harnessing Transparency and Citizen Engagement." Policy Research Report, World Bank, Washington, DC.
———. 2017. *World Development Report 2017: Governance and the Law*. Washington, DC: World Bank.

CHAPTER 2

From Concept to Measurement: Assessment of Policy Areas

Citizen Engagement in Policy Formulation

The extent to which governments inform citizens about upcoming regulations, solicit inputs from them in the drafting of regulations, and assess the effect of proposed regulations on the basis of evidence has an important bearing on the quality of regulatory regimes. Such disciplines in the regulatory design phase have important implications for privilege seeking and vulnerability of policy regimes to such influences. This chapter focuses on an important aspect of policy formulation, that is, the overall process of rule making. Transparency and stakeholder engagement in individual policy areas are analyzed in other sections of this chapter. This macro-analysis is important because transparent and consultative practices in individual policy areas may be short-lived in the absence of an overall government commitment to such practices.

This chapter is based on the 2016 World Bank Global Indicators of Regulatory Governance, which measure citizen engagement in rule making (figure 2.1). This global exercise established benchmarks for more than 180 economies along several dimensions of the regulatory design phase, including (a) prior notification of upcoming regulations and publication of draft regulations; (b) solicitation of comments from citizens on the drafts; (c) reporting of results of the consultations; and (d) carrying out impact assessments of proposed regulations. Prior notice on upcoming regulations reduces regulatory surprises and provides stakeholders with adequate time to prepare for an assessment of the draft regulations when they are published. Accessible publication of drafts and an inclusive consultation process allow a wide range of stakeholders to become aware of the contents and voice their opinion. For example, they can examine whether the regulations, as written, would create opportunities for privilege seeking and, if so, push for more privilege-resistant drafting of regulations.

FIGURE 2.1

Citizen Engagement in Rulemaking in MENA and European, 2015

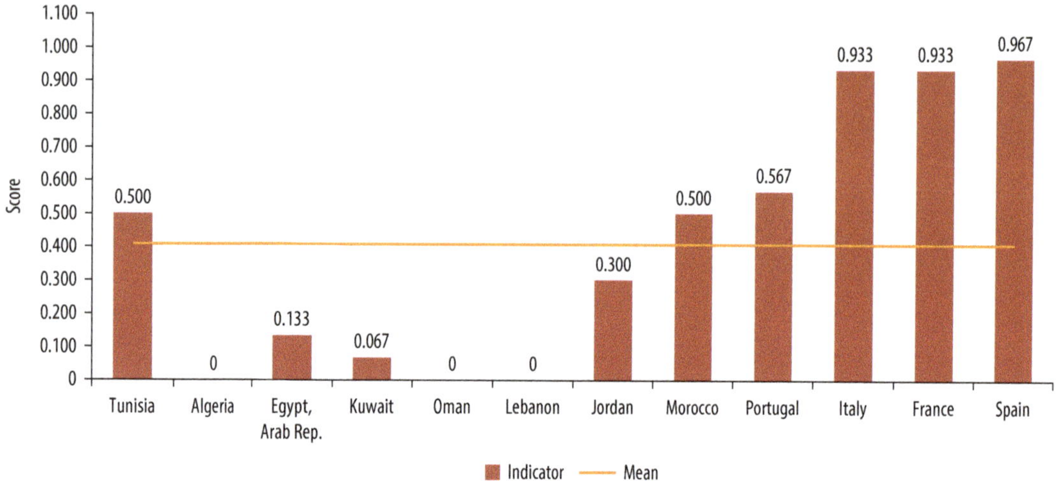

Source: World Bank Global Indicators of Regulary Governance 2016.
Note: MENA = Middle East and North Africa.

These transparency enhancing processes are strengthened if complemented by accountability measures. An important test of a government's commitment to consultative practices is the practice of reporting back on the consultation results. Governments are not expected to incorporate all comments received from stakeholders, especially since comments can be contradictory. However, the requirement to report back enhances accountability. Additional discipline is provided when impact assessments of proposed regulations are conducted. Other things remaining the same, an impact assessment lowers the probability of regulations being written in a way that accords undue privileges to a select few. By taking a thorough look at the outcome and impact chain, such assessments may reveal loopholes that make the proposed regulations vulnerable to privilege seeking.

A high degree of transparency, a commitment to consultation, and the discipline of evidence-based regulatory design are not uncommon in high-income countries. This is shown in figure 2.1, which shows the composite scores from the Global Indicators of Regulatory Governance benchmarking exercise for four high-income European countries (the comparators) and the eight Middle East and North Africa (MENA) countries covered by this study. Although there is some variation among the four comparator countries, the main difference is between the MENA countries and their European comparators—the former predictably performing much worse in engaging citizens in rule making. Also striking is the difference in the MENA region. Two clear groups emerge. Three countries—Morocco and Tunisia in the west and Jordan in the east—score near the average for the entire sample of 12 countries, that is, including the European countries. The other five—Algeria, the Arab Republic of Egypt, Kuwait, Lebanon, and Oman—score very low. In the following sections, we further explore these findings by looking at the individual dimensions of regulatory design.

Prior Notice and the Publication of Drafts

Five countries in the MENA region—Egypt, Jordan, Kuwait, Morocco, and Tunisia—give prior notice of upcoming regulations by publishing their draft text. Of these, Kuwait is the only country that does not publish the entire text of the proposed draft regulation. Algeria, Lebanon, and Oman do not publish the text or summary of proposed regulations before their enactment.

Performance, however, varies among the different countries (see figure 2.2). Morocco is the only country in which the rulemaking body is required by law to give notice and publish draft regulations at least 15 days before enactment. Thus, although in the other four countries ministries or regulatory agencies publish the text or summary of draft regulations, the lack of a legal requirement renders these practices less than robust. In Morocco, Tunisia, and Jordan, the notices and draft regulations are posted on a unified website. In Jordan, draft regulations are also published on a ministry website. Egypt informs citizens through public meetings or direct distribution to interested stakeholders.

In all five countries, with the exception of Kuwait, the entire legal text of the proposed draft is published. Furthermore, anyone can access the text of proposed regulations, except in Egypt and Kuwait. In Morocco,

FIGURE 2.2

Publication of Draft Regulations in MENA, 2015

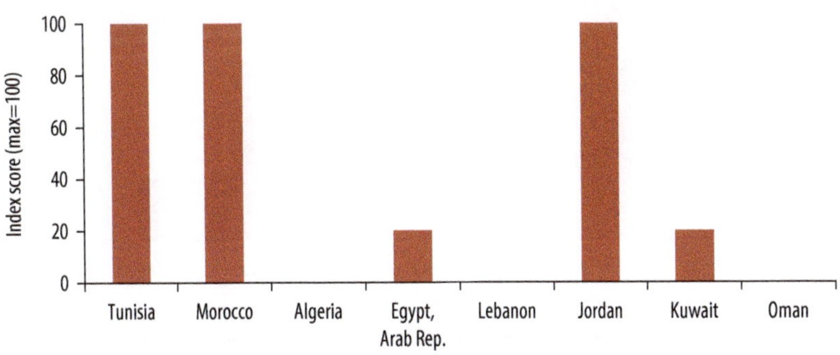

Source: World Bank Global Indicators of Regulary Governance 2016.
Note: MENA = Middle East and North Africa.

the law sets the time period for the proposed text to be available for public consultation. These nuances indicate that even when countries do share draft regulations, the degree of transparency may vary. In this case, for example, while both Egypt and Morocco share drafts, the practice is substantially less transparent in the former (figure 2.2).

Quality of Consultations on Draft Regulations

The degree of stakeholder engagement goes down as we move from the publication of drafts to the quality of consultation on the draft regulations (figure 2.3). In all countries, with the exception of Algeria, Lebanon, and Oman, ministries or regulatory agencies request comments on proposed regulations. In Lebanon, stakeholders do not formally get access to the drafts, and there is no scope for them to shape regulations by providing inputs. However, powerful stakeholders, such as well-connected businesses, may influence rulemaking through informal channels. Because other stakeholders' voices are not heard, there is a greater likelihood that regulations will be framed such that a select few are favored. The situation could even be worse in Oman: given that drafts are not published, less influential stakeholders may be completely unaware of proposed regulations, let alone provide any comments.

Variations exist among countries that seek comments from stakeholders. In only one country, Morocco, the rulemaking body is required by law to request comments, and a specialized government body receives the comments. This somewhat enhances the robustness of the consultation process. There is also variation in the means used to obtain comments.

FIGURE 2.3

Quality of the Consultation Process in MENA, 2015

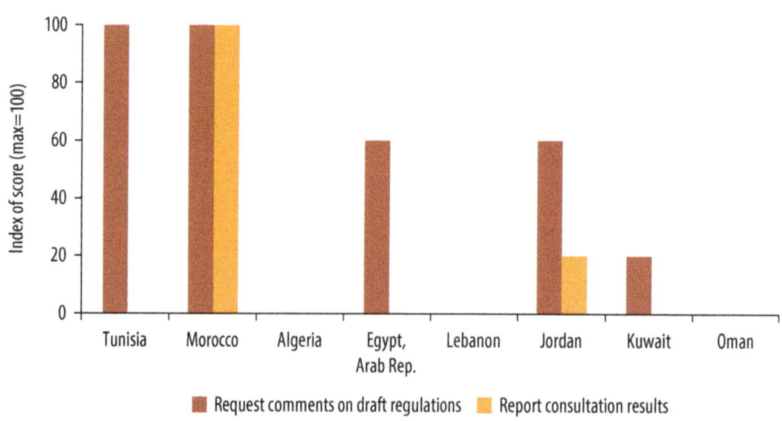

Source: World Bank Global Indicators of Regulary Governance 2016.
Note: MENA = Middle East and North Africa.

Jordan and Egypt, for example, use public meetings and targeted outreach to business associations or other stakeholders (Jordan also uses official correspondence through letters) but they do not have a website through which comments are requested. Tunisia uses a unified website, as does Morocco, and targeted outreach. Kuwait uses only targeted outreach, which could potentially leave out many less influential stakeholders from the consultation process. The practice of conducting public consultation and reporting back on its results across the eight MENA countries is reflected in figure 2.3.

The culture of transparency is strengthened by strong accountability mechanisms. An important measure of accountability is reporting back on the consultations. Such reporting back, even in summary form, reveals the variety of comments and stakeholder concerns and the manner in which the government has responded. This puts pressure on governments to demonstrate that they have addressed the comments adequately. The MENA countries perform very poorly on this score. While five countries invite comments on draft regulations (albeit with many weaknesses in the consultation process), only two, Morocco and Jordan, report back on the results of the consultation (figure 2.3). However, there are weaknesses in Jordan. Unlike in Morocco, reporting back is not required by law, and the reports are not published on a website. Instead, customized responses are provided to certain audiences.

Provision of Impact Assessment

Only Tunisia provides impact assessments of proposed regulations (figure 2.4). In Tunisia, these impact assessments are required by law and conducted only after the consultation. However, the assessments are kept

FIGURE 2.4

Provision of Impact Assessment of Proposed Regulations in MENA, 2015

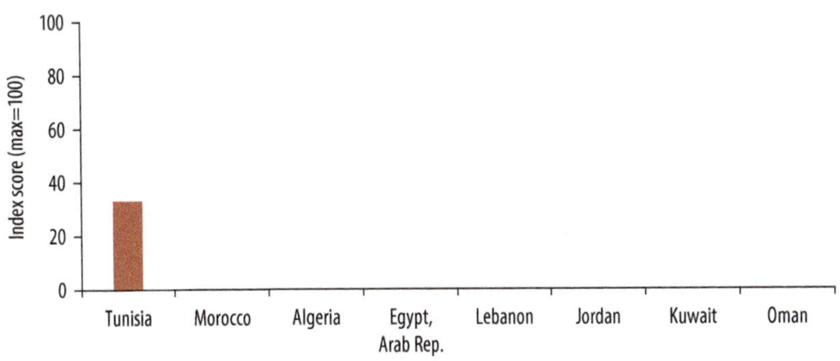

Source: Global Indicators of Regulatory Governance 2016.
Note: MENA = Middle East and North Africa.

internal and are not distributed to the public. Thus, although the assessments typically cover a range of impacts (for example, on the public sector and administrative costs, the environment, and social outcomes, including employment) they may not be good quality.

Conclusion

Countries in the MENA region still need to make improvements in having a transparent and participatory approach to policy making, underpinned by a strong sense of government accountability. There is variation within the region with some pockets of good practice. However, the robustness of such good practices can be questioned.

The country-specific findings suggest a threefold grouping of countries in terms of how they perform on the following dimensions: (a) prior publication of draft regulations, (b) quality of consultations, (c) reporting back on consultations, and (d) carrying out impact assessments.

Morocco and Tunisia appear to have the best performance with several good practices in the first two areas. They need to complement these by improving or initiating the practice of impact assessments of regulations. Tunisia, notably, is the only country that carries out impact assessments of proposed regulations. However, it does not report back at all on consultation results, which is a serious weakness from the point of view of accountability. In addition, there is further scope for improvement in the other three areas. For example, in Tunisia, some of the good practices are not legal requirements unlike in Morocco, where there is a legal requirement to publish draft regulations, request comments, and report on the results of the consultations. The absence of a legal requirement in some instances raises questions about the sustainability of such good practices in Tunisia.

Jordan, Egypt, and Kuwait come next. In terms of the overall score (figure 2.1), these three countries underperform with respect to Morocco and Tunisia, and their performance is also less uniform across the dimensions compared to each other. Jordan does relatively better with regard to publication of draft regulations and (along with Morocco) reports back on the results of consultation. However, it does not conduct impact assessments, which is a detriment to the quality of proposed regulations. Egypt provides notice of upcoming regulations by sharing their text in public meetings and through direct distribution to interested stakeholders. It carries out consultations on proposed regulations but typically in a targeted manner with selected groups.

The other three countries—*Algeria, Lebanon, and Oman*—demonstrate little commitment to transparent and participatory approaches to rule making. Algeria, Lebanon, and Oman score zero on publication of draft regulations. They neither carry out public consultation nor conduct any impact assessment.

These findings provide some preliminary indications of the reform priorities in these countries. For Morocco and Tunisia, the main priority will be to consolidate the good practices that currently exist. Thus, Tunisia should consider putting these practices on a solid legal footing by making them legal requirements. Also both countries should consider introducing or improving the practice of impact assessments. This is a major discipline that is currently weak in both countries. For Jordan, Kuwait, and Egypt, there could be a strategic choice to make. These countries may focus on the areas where they already have some good practices (for example, publishing draft regulations and conducting public consultation) and improve these areas further. An alternative approach would be to focus on areas in which they perform very poorly at present (for example, conducting impact assessments and reporting back on consultation results) and improve their performance in these areas. For Algeria, Lebanon, and Oman, the agenda is much more challenging because of their poor performance across the board. Further analysis is required to come up with an appropriate reform strategy for these countries.

When it comes to enacted regulations currently in force, data show that affected parties can request reconsideration or appeal adopted regulations in only three countries: Jordan, Lebanon, and Tunisia. However, neither of these economies have a requirement in place to periodically review regulations and check whether they are still needed or should be revised. Nevertheless, in all eight MENA countries, current laws and regulations appear to be easily accessible. They are available in a single place, such as on unified websites in Algeria, Jordan, Kuwait, Morocco, and Tunisia. They are also widely printed in official gazettes across the region.

Trade and Customs

Importing and exporting are important operations in the life cycle of a firm, and unfair treatment in the process of importing inputs or exporting goods can be very costly, sometimes threatening the very survival of the business. Thus, an enabling environment for the private sector should guarantee trade and customs policies that are simple and legible, leaving little room for undue discretion that leads to arbitrariness and privileges.

The assessment of trade and customs policies in the selected MENA countries, and their resistance to privilege, covers seven dimensions, as shown in figure 2.1.:

- *Tariff structure and transparency*. The more complex and opaque is the tariff structure, the more room there is for discretionary interpretation, arbitrariness, and privileges, and as the tariffs increase, the more incentive there is to commit fraud and avoid those high tariffs.
- *Import restrictions and special regimes*. As more restrictions and exceptions create rents, there is an increase in incentives to seek privilege as well as opportunities to grant them.[1]
- *Electronic processing of declarations and connectivity*. Electronic processing favors transparency, and clearing procedures available to the public on a web portal are a good way to reduce arbitrariness because every firm knows what it is supposed to pay.
- *Fines and incentives to discover fraud.*
- *Obligation to go through brokers*. They can be intermediaries for corruption.
- *Customs procedures and ethics.*
- *Grievance mechanisms*. These allow for corrective mechanisms in case of unfair treatment.

Before comparing countries, it is important to distinguish the main objectives of customs: revenue collection, trade facilitation, or a controlling function for security reasons. In resource-rich countries of the region, the main objective of customs is not revenue collection but much more a security imperative. Trade facilitation is rarely the main function of customs.

Morocco performs the best and Kuwait the worst in this policy area (figure 2.5). The other five countries (no data are available for Oman) are bunched close together in the overall privilege-resistant score for trade and customs, with their scores ranging from 0.64 to 0.77. Kuwait's performance is uniformly poor across all the broad dimensions covered, but particularly so in terms of tariff structure and transparency (figure 2.5). Its customs do not have a strong fiscal role and do not handle large amounts of trade which can explain its ranking. Morocco, the best performer, has a uniformly good performance but it particularly stands out in the area of trade restrictions and special regimes.

Algerian customs' main objective is not to generate revenues but rather to control borders with a security imperative. In this regard, customs is

TABLE 2.1

Privilege-Resistant Trade and Customs Questionnaire

Tariff structure and transparency	Verifies that tariff data are publicly available and up to date. It also assesses the tariff structure and the room or incentive for cheating the system.
Import restrictions and special regimes	Assess the mechanism for granting import licenses and the existence of clear and transparent criteria as opposed to de facto hidden requirements. They also assess whether physical inspection regimes are burdensome.
Electronic processing of declarations and connectivity	Assesses the degree of electronic processing as opposed to human processing and the electronic centralization of bookkeeping.
Fines	Assess whether the scale of fines is publicly available and whether the fines provide custom agents' incentives for discovering fraud.
Brokers	Assess whether brokers could be agents of corruption.
Customs procedures and ethics	Assess the quality of customs' internal procedures and sanctions for corruption.
Laws and appeals	Verify whether it is possible to appeal decisions in a specified time frame and with and independent jurisdiction.

FIGURE 2.5

Privilege Resistance in Trade and Customs in MENA, 2015

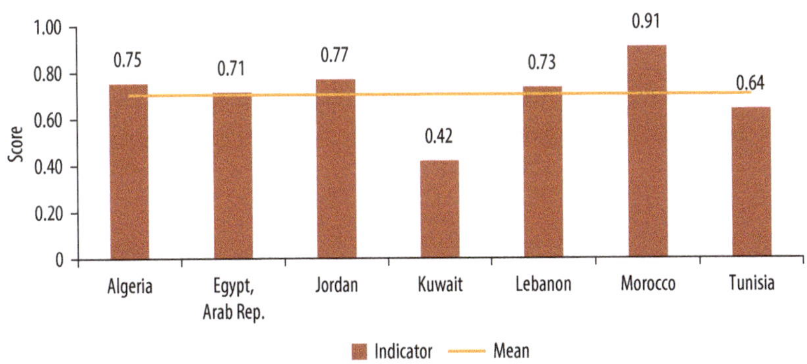

Note: MENA = Middle East and North Africa.

better equipped than its counterparts in the region, with headquarters connected to the main border posts, regulations in place, and enforced relatively well with a well-functioning internal sanctions and appeal mechanisms. However, this well-functioning administration does not seem to pay much attention to service delivery to the private sector by requiring paper declaration and not making public, for instance, the scale of infringement. Moreover, a recent decision by the government to introduce new import licenses (probably because of a protection imperative) with no clear criteria for granting them opens the door to arbitrariness and privileges.

Among customs agencies for which revenue collection has been a major objective, Tunisia ranks particularly low. It faces major possibilities for privileges and special treatments due to an increased lack of discipline, poor grievance mechanisms, and cronyism in recent years (Rijkers, Freund, and Nucifora 2014). Two other countries ranking in the middle, Lebanon and Egypt, have room for improvement in terms of transparency as well as reducing bargaining power of officials to grant import licenses, especially given that Lebanon is known for institutionalized privileges in terms of import licenses.

Tariff Structure and Transparency

Moving on to specific dimensions of the trade and customs regime, Egypt exemplifies a common pattern in the region with regard to tariff structure and transparency (figure 2.6). It has a large number (12) of tariff bands and high tariff peaks. The multiplicity and complexity of tariff bands leave room for interpretation and discretion from the customs authority, and increases the incentive for private firms to game the system.

Import Restrictions and Special Regimes

Tunisia's customs regime exemplifies poor performance on another dimension, that is, import restrictions and special regimes (figure 2.7).

FIGURE 2.6

Tariff Structure and Transparency in MENA, 2015

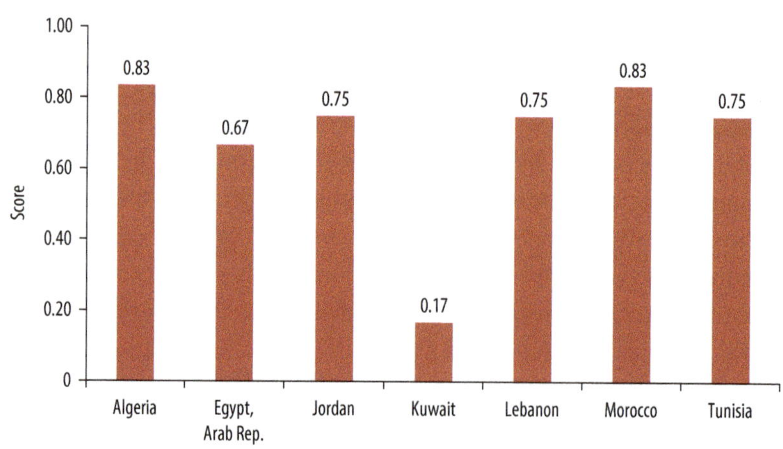

Note: MENA = Middle East and North Africa.

FIGURE 2.7

Import Restrictions and Special Regimes in MENA, 2015

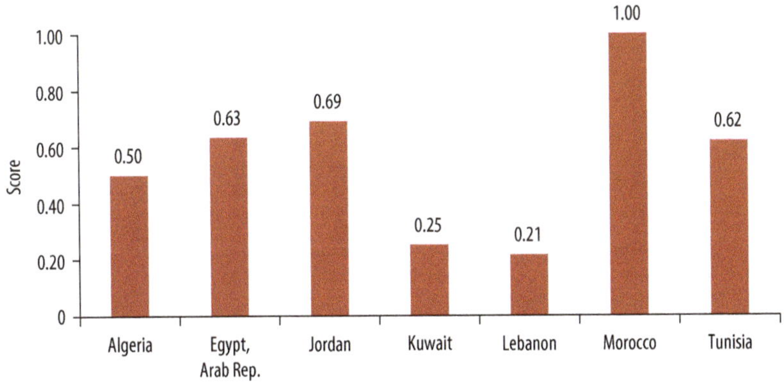

Note: MENA = Middle East and North Africa.

It is characterized by the existence of nonautomatic licenses and numerous import regimes, which leave much room for privileges and possible collusion.[2] Moreover, Tunisia is deficient in making public the complex import processes. Appeals against customs decisions are nonexistent in practice despite their possibility on paper. Moreover, sanctions in customs and among brokers for noncompliance or collusion have been virtually nonexistent in the past few years—only one custom agent was sanctioned in the last four years and no broker license was removed in the past five years—despite well-known increase in customs fraud (Ayadi et al. 2013). Import processes are complex and have built-in leeway for negotiations. Therefore, in a context of low discipline, fraud and smuggling have started to prosper. After implementing important reforms before the revolution (but colluding with the Ben Ali family to a large extent; see Rijkers, Freund, and Nucifora 2014), Tunisian customs has deteriorated significantly after the revolution, crippled with increasing corruption and collusion.[3]

Electronic Processing and Connectivity

In terms of electronic processing and connectivity (figure 2.8), Tunisia ranks at the bottom with Kuwait. The absence of electronic processing of customs declarations is another loophole that opens the door to human interaction, arbitrariness, discretion, and even corruption. Absence of connectivity between customs offices leads to less scrutiny and control on crony firms' transactions and operations. Morocco performs moderately well on this dimension but does not stand out. Although it has

FIGURE 2.8

Electronic Processing and Connectivity in MENA, 2015

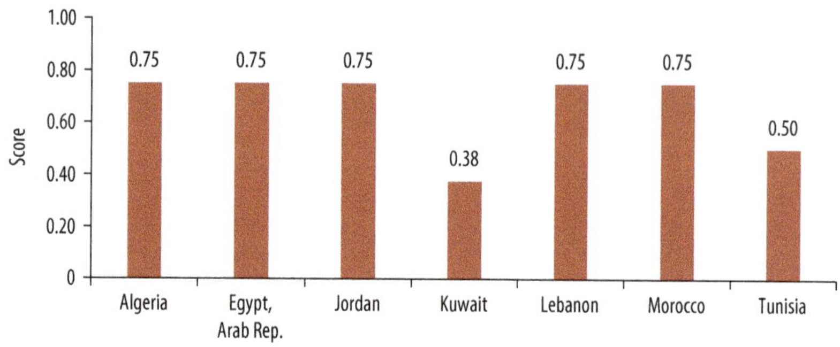

Note: MENA = Middle East and North Africa.

successfully carried out customs reform to increase transparency, scrutiny, and grievance mechanisms, the reform agenda is unfinished. Reforms are required to phase out paper declarations, increase transparency, and work on custom agents' incentives and behaviors to curb fraud and corruption.

Business Regulation Practices

Business surveys indicate that regulatory policy uncertainty is a major constraint faced by entrepreneurs in the MENA region. World Bank (2015d) has argued that discriminatory implementation of policy, especially undue discretion in enforcing rules and regulations, is a major reason why businesses in the region perceive policy uncertainty. The report provides results from an analysis of the variations in time taken to complete different regulatory compliance functions such as clearing goods through customs, or obtaining an operating license or a construction permit. The data, which cover the period 2006–13, show widespread variations in business experience with the same regulatory interface within a country; indeed, within-country variations are greater than differences across countries.

Weaknesses in the business regulatory regime create scope for the discretionary enforcement of regulations. This section assesses such weaknesses in the MENA region. It does not aspire to provide a comprehensive assessment of the privilege resistance of all such areas. Rather, it is based on data collected for three areas that are important from a firm's point of view and exemplify characteristics of the business regulation regimes in

TABLE 2.2

Privilege-Resistant Business Regulation Questionnaire

Business registration	Verifies that the requirements and fees for obtaining business registration are publicized and there are no hidden or informal ones.
Permits and licenses: construction permits	Verify that the requirements, time frames, and fees for obtaining construction permits are publicized and there are no hidden or informal ones. They also verify whether negative decisions are justified and appeal mechanisms are in place.
Tax inspections	Verify whether tax inspections are risk-based and announced (dates and purpose) and that the tax compliance requirements are publicized. They verify whether tax inspectors behave transparently and are accountable for their actions and whether appeal mechanisms are in place.

the countries studied. The areas are (a) business registration, (b) obtaining construction permit (proxy for the permitting and licensing regime), and (c) tax inspections.[4]

These areas relate to different parts of the life cycle of a business. *Business registration* is essentially an entry requirement, although in many countries registration needs to be renewed at regular intervals during a firm's operations. *Obtaining a construction permit* is relevant to both the entry and operations stages. Unless a firm is operating from a rented premise, one of the first things it needs to do is construct a factory or office premise. Moreover, additional construction work is often required during the lifetime of a business, especially for those expanding their operations. A *tax inspection* is a regulatory interface that is largely and frequently encountered during operations.

These features of the three business regulation interfaces influence the degree to which businesses are vulnerable to regulatory harassment. We may consider a "vulnerability" indicator based on two factors: (a) the cost to businesses of an adverse decision by the regulator, and (b) the probability of such an adverse decision that, in turn, depends on the frequency of the regulatory interface and the intrinsic scope for discretionary interpretation by government officials.[5] By this definition, the degree of vulnerability is likely to be lowest for business registration, highest for tax inspections, and in-between for construction permitting. This is because the frequency of the interface, as well as the scope for discretionary interpretation of a business's regulatory compliance and its operating conditions (such as taxable profits), is lowest for business registration and highest for tax inspections. The costs of business interruption or shutdown because of an adverse government decision are likely to be greater when a business is operational (most relevant for tax inspections) than when it has yet to start operations (relevant for business registration). Construction permitting lies between these aspects.

A flip side is the degree to which influential businesses may benefit from manipulating the system. Such businesses have more at stake with the tax regime than with the business registration process, with construction permitting falling in-between. Thus the "incentive to capture" measure will go up progressively from business registration to construction permitting to tax inspections. Figure 2.9 summarizes this logical chain.

The findings on the business regulation interface are quite revealing. Figure 2.10 summarizes the scores for each of the three regulatory interfaces, with a higher score signifying greater privilege resistance of the interface. For the MENA countries, the quality deteriorates progressively from business regulations to construction permitting to tax inspections. The actual opportunity for capture by influential businesses and the likelihood of harassment of ordinary businesses are highest in the very areas in which the intrinsic "incentive to capture" and "vulnerability

FIGURE 2.9

Policy to Privilege Chain

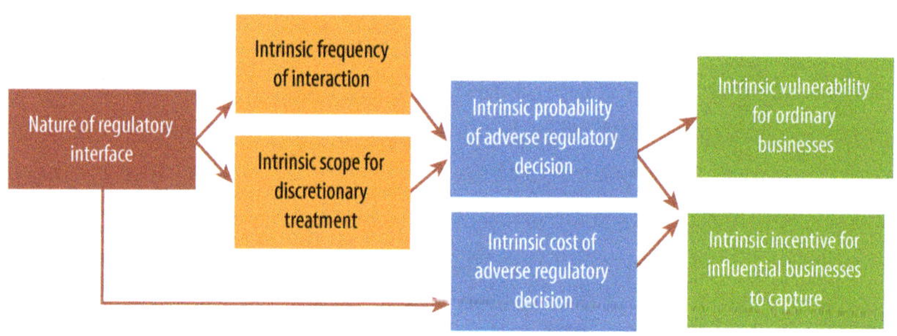

FIGURE 2.10

Privilege Resistance for Business Regulation Interfaces in MENA and European Comparators, 2015

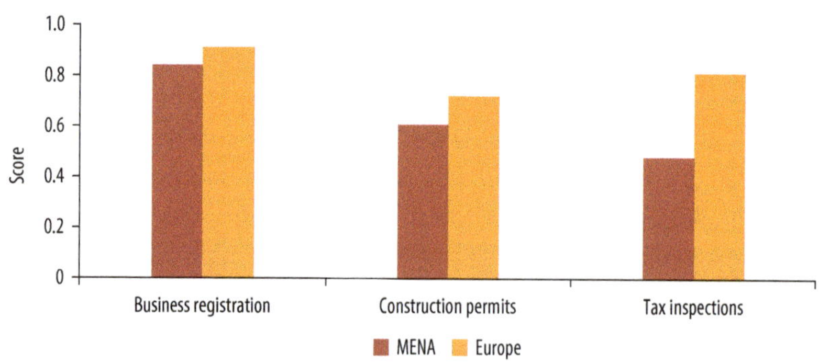

Note: A higher score means greater privilege resistance. Europe is here represented by Italy, France, Portugal, and Spain. MENA = Middle East and North Africa.

to harassment" is highest (that is, tax inspections)—in other words, a double jeopardy.

The intrinsic measures are a function of the type of regulatory interface and should not vary much between countries. Governments can counteract the intrinsic nature of the regulatory interface (especially when it is adverse) by policy decisions that shape the actual nature of the regulatory interface. Thus, governments should make privilege resistant those regulatory regimes that are intrinsically more problematic, such as tax inspections. In the MENA region, the opposite seems to have happened.

Differences within MENA

The general picture hides variations across the region. Lebanon, Kuwait, and Tunisia rank at the bottom for their business regulation practices (figure 2.11). Lebanon scores the lowest because of the hidden and informal requirements needed for business registration; the nonpublicity of requirements, fees, and procedures needed for a construction permit; and the need to renew the latter annually with no specified time to obtain the permit, nor a justification for a negative decision or the possibility to appeal such negative decision. The tax inspection system is not risk-based, the compliance requirements are not publicized, and the firms are not provided copies of the inspection nor able to fill in a complaint.

In Tunisia, tax inspections are not risk-based and the tax compliance requirements are not publicized. Tax enforcement decisions are not

FIGURE 2.11

Business Regulation Indicator Scores in MENA and European Comparators, 2015

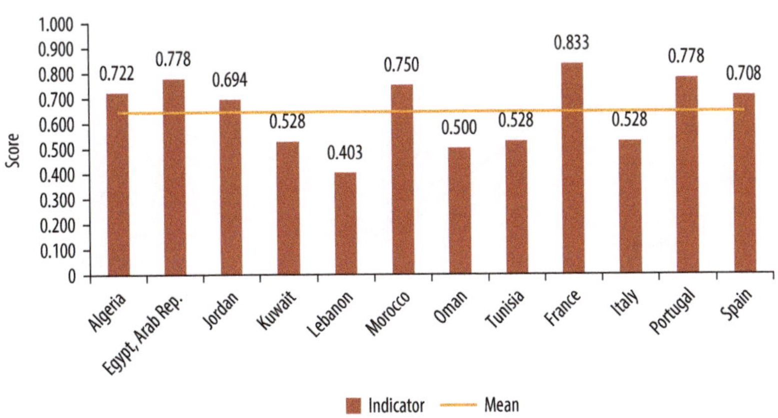

Note: MENA = Middle East and North Africa.

vetted by a commission or supervisor, leaving the power in the hands of a sole tax inspector who can then threaten a firm with suspension and extract a bribe. As in Lebanon, there are no grievance mechanisms for tax inspections. In Kuwait, construction permits are not delivered in a specified time frame, and firms are unable to appeal a negative decision. Kuwait's tax inspection profile is similar to that of Lebanon.

Algeria, Morocco, and Jordan rank in the middle displaying some gaps. For instance, Algeria and Morocco have hidden fees for obtaining construction permits. In Jordan, tax inspectors have too much power, business registration involves hidden requirements and fees, and there is an opaque procedure—with no specified time frame—for obtaining construction permits.

While some countries perform well based on the average of the three regulatory interfaces, there are significant differences within-country across regulatory areas (see figure 2.12). Egypt is a good example.

FIGURE 2.12

Business Regulation Dimension Scores in MENA, 2015

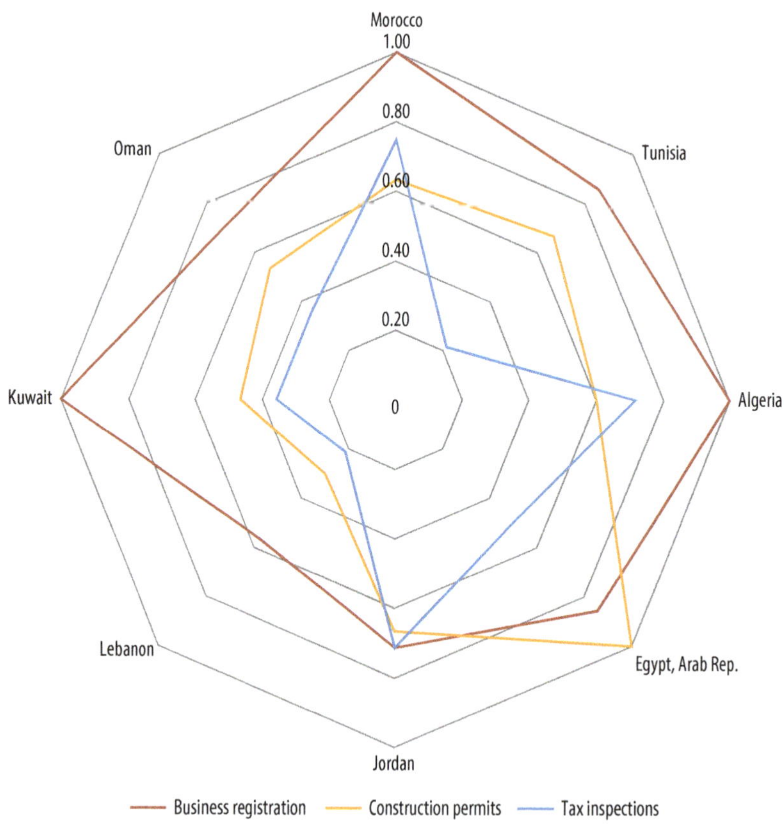

Note: MENA = Middle East and North Africa.

Overall, Egypt outperforms its neighbors in terms of the transparency and fairness of its business regulation practices, except that business registration needs to be renewed every five years. This requirement multiplies the points of contact with the administration and increases opportunities for extracting bribes by threatening the continuity of the business. However, Egypt scores rather poorly on the tax transparency score. Tax inspectors, for example, have considerable power to suspend a business and are not required to provide copies of tax inspections.

Jordan provides a contrast. Its overall score is not stellar; it comes fourth best after Egypt, Morocco, and Algeria. However, there is much less variation, with the scores being roughly the same for the individual business regulation areas. While not as low as in Jordan, the variation across the three regulatory areas is moderate in Algeria and Morocco. High variation across regulatory areas, as in Egypt and some of the other countries, can be a warning sign since significantly nontransparent practices in an area can contaminate areas in which the practices are transparent for now.

Public Procurement

Public procurement accounts for one-fifth of the global gross domestic product (GDP) (World Bank 2016b). In middle-income countries, about half of public spending goes to the purchase of goods and services. Therefore, it is an important point of contact and interaction between the state and the private sector, and an essential source of business for many private firms including small and medium enterprises (SMEs). This interaction with the administration can lend itself to privileges and capture, favoring some firms over others on unfair grounds and thereby diverting public funds for private gains.

Five aspects of public procurement policies and practices are covered and assessed in this section: (a) the institutional and regulatory framework governing public procurement; (b) fair opportunity and equality of treatment; (c) transparency, confidentiality, and access to information; (d) existence and fairness of grievance mechanisms; and (e) transparency, integrity, and accountability of the procurement system.

The pillars used to assess the fairness and privilege resistance of public procurement systems are partly based on the OECD MAPS methodology (OECD 2010), which is an auto-assessment tool for countries aiming to improve their procurement system. The framework of this report focuses on the governance aspects of the public procurement system rather than on its operational efficiency, and is an external (as opposed to an auto-) assessment by experts of regulations and practices.

TABLE 2.3

Privilege-Resistant Procurement Questionnaire

Institutional and regulatory frameworks	Verify the existence of a regulatory body that has its own budget and is by law and in practice not involved in procurement operations (free of conflict of interest); are part of institutionalization of a multiyear procurement planning exercise in support of budget planning.
Fair opportunity	Verifies that procurement opportunities are widely publicized and no large preference is granted to bidders over others; the clarity of qualification criteria; and the existence of methodologies to evaluate technical and price capacities of bids.
Transparency, confidentiality, and access to information	Verify that public opening of tenders follows a defined, regulated, transparent, secure, and confidential process.
Grievance, complaint, recourse	Verify that bidders have the right to appeal a procurement decision and ask for an independent review and obtain a decision in an established time frame.
Integrity and accountability	Verify that fraud, corruption, conflict of interest, unethical behavior, and their consequences are considered in the regulatory framework for procurement.

FIGURE 2.13

Public Procurement Privilege Resistance Scores in MENA, 2015

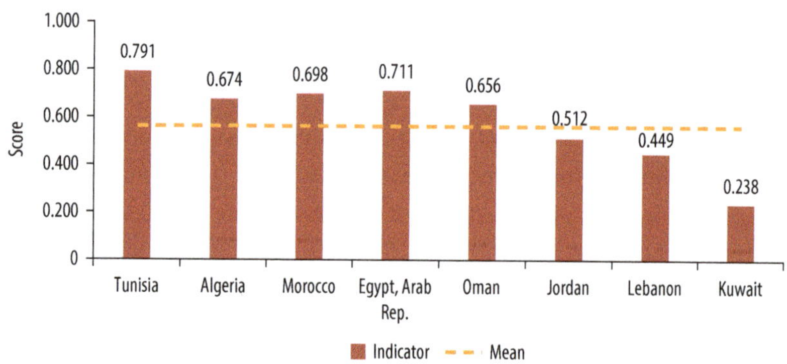

Note: MENA = Middle East and North Africa.

There is wide variation in the degree to which the public procurement regime is vulnerable to privilege seeking ranging from a reasonably robust regime in Tunisia to a very vulnerable procurement regime in Kuwait (figure 2.13). Nonetheless, all countries have weaknesses in one or more dimensions of the procurement regime.

Institutional Framework Governing Public Procurement

A good practice for an institutional framework governing public procurement is to have a dedicated regulatory body or authority overseeing public procurement. This entity has to be independent from political influence and possess its own budget. It also has to be free from any involvement in procurement operations and planning to avoid any conflicts of interest.

Only Morocco, Tunisia, Egypt, and Oman have a regulatory body or an authority that oversees public procurement. However, their effectiveness is likely to vary. In Algeria, there is no authority in charge of public procurement. However, the procurement law and the processes in place are so strong that they lead to the same score as a country with an authority in charge of public procurement. Here, the function took precedence over the form since the duties of such institution are performed given the strong legal framework and processes in place.

In Egypt and Oman, the authorities have their own budget but their counterparts in Morocco and Tunisia do not. On the other hand, the authority in Morocco is prohibited, both by regulation and in practice, from participating in procurement planning, procurement activities, and evaluation of bids. This serves to enhance its neutrality. The same is true for Egypt, but partially. The authorities in Tunisia and Oman are not subject to such prohibitions.

Lebanon, Jordan, and Kuwait do not have a regulatory body or authority to oversee public procurement. Lebanon is in the process of reinstating a high tender board. In Jordan, procurement activity by the central government is largely carried out by three entities: the Ministry of Work's General Tender Directorate (for construction procurement), the Ministry of Finance's General Supply Department (for purchase of goods) and the Joint Procurement Directorate attached to the Office of the Prime Minister (for purchase of medicine). Despite being on the reform agenda for many years, an initiative to merge these entities into a central oversight unit has not materialized. There is also no entity in charge of a common regulatory framework, and each of the three procurement entities are responsible for their own regulations (World Bank 2015b).

Fair Opportunity

In terms of fair opportunity, procurement opportunities should be widely and transparently advertised to ensure equal opportunity of access to all bidders. With the exception of Lebanon, the MENA countries favor national companies formally through the law. For instance, in Tunisia, offers submitted by Tunisian companies (in public works contracts as well as the Tunisian products in all markets to supply goods) would be preferred to offers from foreign firms and products of any origin other than Tunisian, whenever such services and products are of equal quality, and as long as the price of Tunisian products does not exceed more than 10 percent of the amount of the offers of foreign companies and the prices of foreign goods (Benchmarking Public Procurement 2017). In Algeria, a quota of procurement contracts must be awarded to domestic firms. A margin of preference of 25 percent is granted to Algerian products or companies owned mainly by Algerian nationals. Moreover, if a need or service can be met by a micro-enterprise, the contracting services is required to procure it from a micro-enterprise. In Egypt the margin is 15 percent of the price.

In Kuwait, Egypt, Jordan, and Lebanon (where state-owned enterprises [SOEs] do not participate in bids) the public procurement framework does not favor SOEs, whereas in Algeria, Tunisia, Morocco, and Oman it does. This poses competition issues and constrains the ability of the private sector to benefit from public procurement opportunities.

All countries have a regulatory framework that requires that procurement opportunities (other than sole source or price quotations) be publicly advertised in a national gazette or a widely distributed newspaper. It is also the case regarding advertisement on a central web portal with different degrees of accessibility to the relevant information.

Transparency, Confidentiality, and Access to Information

In terms of *transparency, confidentiality, and access to information*, public opening of tenders should follow a defined, secure, confidential, and regulated procedure that is predictable and known by all parties, ideally in the 24 hours after the closing date for bid submission. Records of proceedings for bid openings should be retained and available for review.

Another good practice is the existence of an integrated information system that provides at a minimum, up-to-date procurement information, including tender invitations and requests for proposals. Such information systems should be accessible to the public at no or minimum cost. Tender decisions and modifications should be publicly available (such as on a government website or national gazette) to provide equal access to information, and thus equal opportunities, to all parties. Such features avoid opacity and hidden manipulation of the procurement process that could unfairly benefit connected firms.

In terms of the aforementioned criteria, Tunisia scores very high fulfilling all the requirements, followed by Egypt and Morocco. For instance, in Morocco, tender documents are accessible for free. In Algeria, there is a cost of US$139 (Benchmarking Public Procurement 2017). In Tunisia, the fee is subject to the discretion of the procuring entity. In Morocco and Tunisia, bidders have the opportunity to ask a question for clarification to the procuring entity and the answers are made available to all interested bidders. In Algeria, bidders cannot ask clarification questions. In Algeria, unsuccessful bidders are not individually notified by the procuring entity that they did not win the contract award. In Tunisia and Morocco, they are notified.

Grievance, Complaint, and Recourse

Grievance, complaint, and recourse mechanisms constitute another dimension that is key to shield public procurement from privileges and corruption by (a) granting the right for a review by an independent review body and (b) by guaranteeing time frames for the issuance of decisions by the procuring agency as well as by the independent review body. The grievance framework is very important since its shortcomings undermine the benefits of regulations that favor transparency and fair treatment since firms cannot obtain redress in case of irregularities.

Morocco, Kuwait, Lebanon, and Jordan score very low. In Jordan, the complaining party does not have the option of filing a complaint.

Integrity and Accountability

Integrity and accountability is the fifth dimension against which we assess the public procurement systems in MENA. This dimension helps lower the prevalence of fraud and corruption by introducing a regulatory framework that includes provisions regarding fraud, corruption, and unethical behavior as well as coercive measures against them.

Jordan's public procurement framework displays high integrity and accountability scores, followed by Algeria and Tunisia. At the bottom, Kuwait and Lebanon lack a regulatory framework that covers fraud and corruption or spells out the individual responsibilities. Both Lebanon and Kuwait lack a confidential system for the public reporting of fraud cases, unethical behavior, and corruption.

Conclusion

In general, Maghreb countries perform well with Tunisia, Algeria, and Morocco being in the top three in terms of the resistance of their public procurement systems to privileges. Nonetheless, some weaknesses in these countries may open the door to privileges and, once that happens, there is a risk that other areas that are fairly robust now may be compromised (see figure 2.14, which shows divergence of performance within and across countries). Thus, while Tunisia is the best performer overall, its institutional framework remains weak. Although there is a regulatory body or authority that oversees public procurement, it does not have

FIGURE 2.14

Public Procurement Policy Scores in MENA, 2015

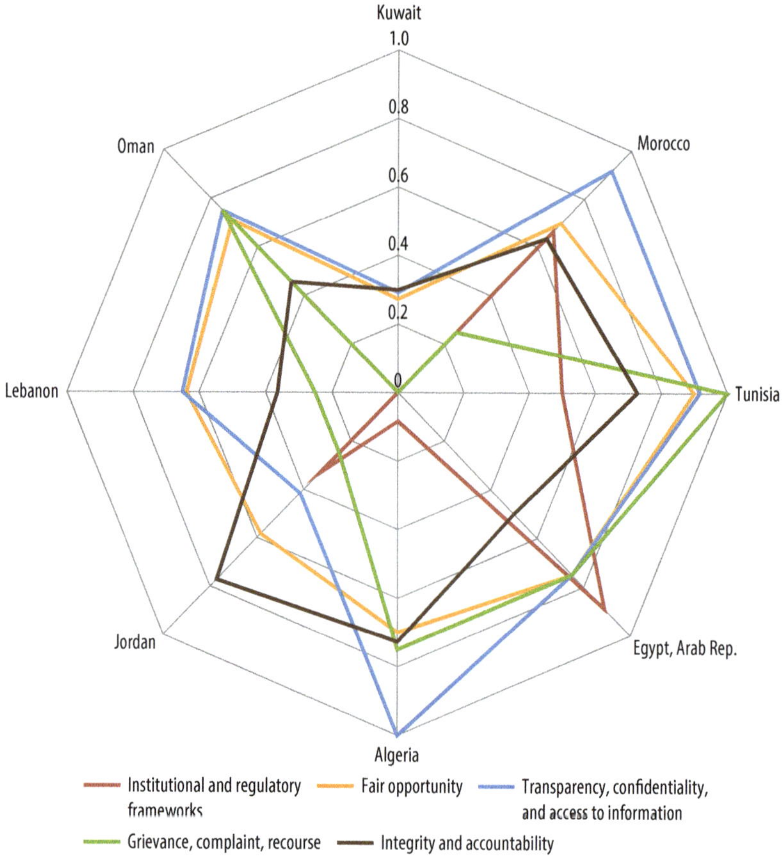

Note: MENA = Middle East and North Africa.

its own budget and its involvement in procurement activities and planning are not prohibited. This may potentially leave room for conflict of interest and privileges.

Morocco, while performing well on four dimensions, has a very poor score on grievance and recourse mechanisms. The lack of effective grievance mechanisms may embolden actors who seek to obtain or provide privileges because unfair treatment to others may go unnoticed in the absence of complaints. Algeria has a similar weakness as Tunisia in the institutional and regulatory framework, but its performance on this front is far worse. The remaining countries also show variations along the five dimensions of the procurement regime, although it is less pronounced for Egypt. Kuwait also shows less variation but only because its performance is uniformly poor.

Performance also diverges when viewed from another angle, that is, within the five dimensions rather than within countries (figure 2.14). For example, with regard to the institutional and regulatory framework, the scores vary from a high of 0.9 (Egypt) to a low of zero (Kuwait). Similarly, in the case of grievance, complaint, and recourse, Tunisia, as the top performer, scores 1; Kuwait scores zero; and Jordan, Lebanon, and Morocco tied near the bottom with a score of 0.25.

These divergences suggest that there is considerable scope for learning from good practices, both across countries on any particular dimension of the procurement regime and within a country across different procurement dimensions. However, variations within countries indicate potential vulnerabilities because good practices in some aspects of the regime may be undone if weaknesses remain in other areas.

Allocation of Public Land

Access to land is crucial for industrial and commercial investment whether it is to build a factory or real estate and tourism projects. When land governance systems are weak, privileges and rent seeking are widespread, thereby leading to inefficient and costly allocation of land to connected investors who may not make the best use of it. In an effort to spur investment and private sector development, governments need to ensure fair, timely, and cost-effective access to public land for investment purposes, providing an efficient and equitable access for all private sector players as part of an efficient and equitable investment climate.

In the MENA region, the land governance framework is reputed to be weak and institutional reforms are needed to bring efficiency and transparency in the process of public land allocation to the private sector.

TABLE 2.4

Privilege-Resistant Land Allocation Questionnaire

Institutional and regulatory framework for public industrial land	Verifies the existence of a public industrial land allocation system and a dedicated, independent management authority. It also assesses the land allocation mechanisms.
Transparency, publicity, and scrutiny	Verify whether reports of allocated land, land inventory, and valuation rolls are made available to the public as well as the quality of the cadaster and land mapping.
Grievance and recourse	Verify if negative decisions are justified and if appeals are possible and managed by an independent body and handled in a specified time frame.
Enforcement: tax collection	Verifies if tax collection is enforced and whether exemptions are based on publicized criteria and applied in a transparent and consistent manner.

To analyze the seven MENA countries,[6] this report uses the World Bank Land Governance Assessment Framework selectively through the lenses of transparency, fairness, and equity as opposed to opacity, discretion, and privileges. Four aspects of public land allocation systems were assessed:

- *The institutional and legal framework* to assess whether a dedicated and independent authority manages land allocation and whether it follows a fair process
- *Transparency, access to information, and integrity of the cadaster*
- *Grievance mechanisms*, that is, the ability to appeal a negative decision
- *Enforcement of tax collection* to assess whether firms are equal in terms of paying their taxes or whether exemptions and special treatments are prevalent

Overall Findings

Overall, land policies in MENA are imperfect. This is equally so across the countries studied, as illustrated by the weak scores that are rather tightly gathered around a low mean.

Algeria ranks at the top in terms of the privilege resistance of its land policies, followed by Tunisia and Jordan (figure 2.15). Thanks to its new cadaster and recently modernized land registry, Lebanon scores better than Kuwait, Egypt, and Morocco.

Institutional and Regulatory Framework for Public Industrial Land

In terms of institutional framework, countries display a reasonable score with the exception of Kuwait (figure 2.16). All covered countries except Kuwait have a dedicated entity in charge of public land allocation. However, this entity is not independent. Public land is allocated through auctions, tenders, cost-benefit analysis, and due diligence processes. In Egypt, however, some lands maybe allocated by virtue of a decree from the competent authority such as the Governorate or the New Urban Communities Authority (NUCA) that may allocate lands in any way it deems necessary.

In general, the assessment of land is not based on market values in Morocco, Algeria, Tunisia, and Kuwait, whereas it is the case in Jordan and Egypt and Lebanon. However, there is certain latitude in the case of Lebanon for the registrar to modify those prices (15 percent of the value), which leaves room for discretion and hence corruption and privileges. Furthermore, in Lebanon and Egypt, land categories are reputed to be

FIGURE 2.15

Privilege Resistance of Land Policies in MENA, 2015

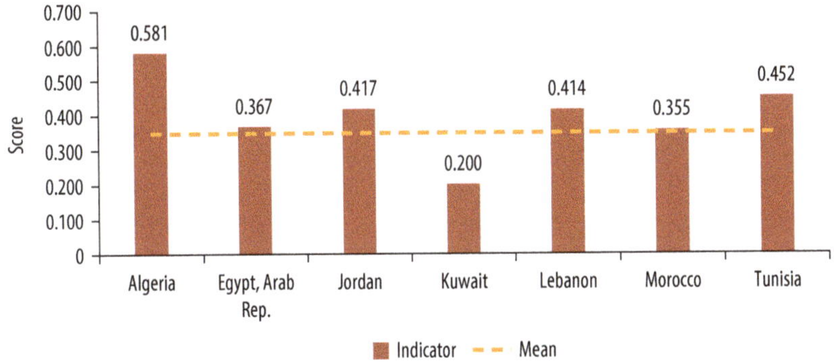

Note: MENA = Middle East and North Africa.

FIGURE 2.16

Institutional and Regulatory Land Policy Frameworks in MENA, 2015

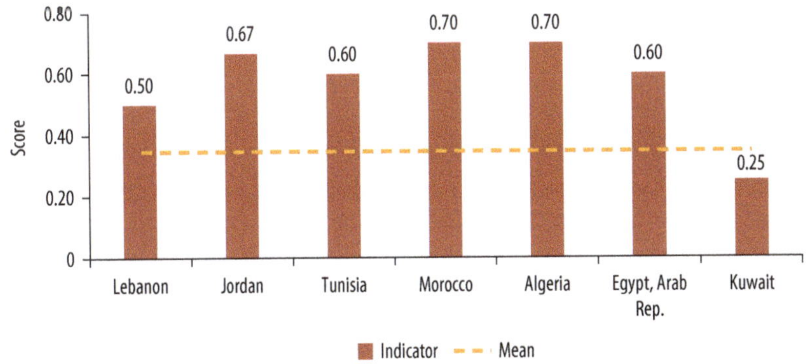

Note: MENA = Middle East and North Africa.

easily changeable. This could reflect, in theory at least, a flexible system in which land categories adapt to the needs of the economy. However, this could also create opportunities for connected elites to obtain agricultural land, for instance, at low prices and then be granted a change of land category to industrial, real estate, or tourism purposes allowing for higher profits.

Transparency and Access to Information

In terms of transparency and access to information, no country in the sample publishes a report of allocated public land every year.

FIGURE 2.17

Transparency, Publicity, and Scrutiny of Land Policies in MENA, 2015

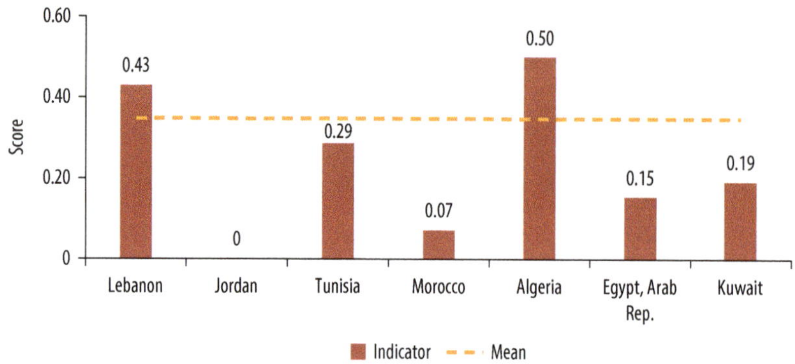

Note: MENA = Middle East and North Africa.

Although not classified as confidential in some countries, such as Jordan, only parties to a transaction are allowed access to the records for the allocated land. This is problematic in terms of publicizing the terms of the allocation and ensuring that the land is used for the stated purpose. In all countries, information on allocated land, available land, and valuation roles is not accessible to the public. Jordan, Kuwait, Morocco, and Egypt rank at the bottom (figure 2.17) since in addition to their lack of transparency, they do not possess functional cadaster and land registry systems. The cadaster and valuation rolls systems are functional in only three countries: Lebanon (following the modernization of the cadaster, although 40 percent of Lebanon is not surveyed yet), Tunisia, and Algeria, in which the land is inventoried and mapped in an up-to-date system. Thus, on the transparency criteria, Algeria ranks at the top followed by Lebanon and Tunisia.

Grievance and Recourse Mechanisms

In terms of **grievance and recourse mechanisms**, Jordan and Morocco score at the top, as shown by figure 2.18, since they offer the possibility of appeal to an independent body. Jordan's appeal body is even required to render a decision within a specified time frame. Algeria, Tunisia, and Egypt offer a possibility of appeal but the appeal body is not independent. Lebanon does not offer the possibility of appeal at all, and in Egypt, the possibility of appeal exists although the land authority is not forced by law to provide arguments and explanations when it renders

FIGURE 2.18

Grievance and Recourse in Land Policies in MENA, 2015

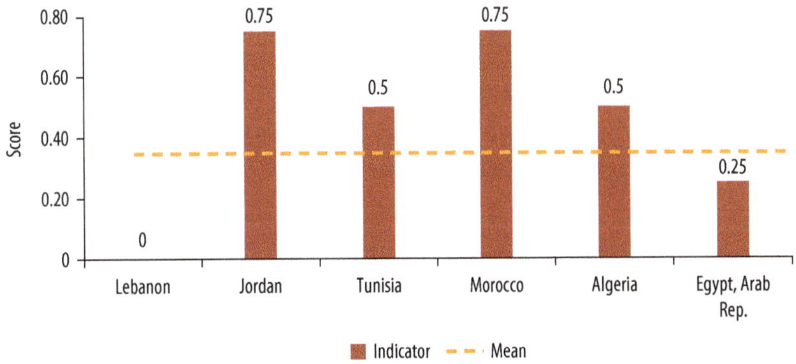

Note: MENA = Middle East and North Africa.

BOX 2.1

Success Story of Public Land Allocation in China

China: Shenzhen SEZ as a policy reform incubator for urban land market development

Public land allocation in China used to be discretionary and inefficient thereby leaving the door open to rent seeking. Despite the fact that Shenzhen has made efforts to improve its land allocation procedures, the issue of privileges and abuse of power persisted. Shenzhen decided to move to a public auction system. China's first state land auction took place on December 1, 1987, in Shenzhen Municipal Hall.

The new competitive land allocation system brought transparency and efficiency to the system, which allowed for more revenues for the municipality. The new system is a radical change from the past when land transfers depended on negotiation and the process was time-consuming and unpredictable. With no reliable market data, land valuation was extremely difficult.

With the new system, Shenzhen land officials could finally pass on the valuation risk to the market, which ended a situation in which connected elites obtained a land that they didn't have the capital to develop, depriving investors the ability to truly able to develop the land and thereby diverting public land from an efficient allocation.

"Thus began what became a popular saying as such reforms later proceeded throughout China: don't go to the shizhang (the mayor), go to the shichang (the market)." It took the national government 15 years to include the competitive land allocation in the law.

Source: Shen and Sun 2012.

a negative decision. In Egypt, Jordan, Algeria, and Morocco, appeals are handled through courts.

In terms of tax collection and enforcement, all property holders are liable for tax and listed on the tax roll except in Jordan and Morocco. The latter ranks at the bottom on this criterion having no clear or publicized criteria for land tax exemption.

An illustration of a virtuous process that revolutionized land allocation is China's Schenzhen special economic zone (see box 2.1.)

Investment Incentives

Well-connected businesses often try to tilt the award of investment incentives in their favor and succeed, even though that may not serve an economic objective of the country. Their ability to do so depends on several factors, of which the nature of the incentive policy regime, including its administration, is among the most important. This section assesses several important dimensions of the incentive policy regime in eight MENA countries in terms of their vulnerability to privilege seeking.

Policy Framework for Incentives

The first set of variables relate to government policy on incentives. The lack of a good policy framework increases the likelihood of discretionary award of incentives. A good incentive policy would clearly articulate the principles of the award process and have provisions for publishing information on the incentives offered. In addition, there should be provision for periodic government review of the incentive regime to assess the results and reform the regime if needed. The first two provisions are intended to introduce transparency to the award process and thereby constrain the ability to covertly award incentives on a purely discretionary basis. The last two provisions may help guard against the perpetuation of a flawed incentive regime or a regime that may have outlived its purpose.

Of the eight countries covered, two—Jordan and Oman—do not have an incentive policy that clearly and publicly states the objectives of the incentives regime. The other six countries have such a policy but often lack good practice provisions. Morocco and Kuwait do quite well, having all the four provisions. Egypt and Tunisia come next with a score of 3 out of 4. Egypt does not have a provision for the reform of the regime, even though the policy provides for periodic reviews, while Tunisia does not provide for publication of information on incentives. Algeria's policy

TABLE 2.5

Privilege-Resistant Incentive Policies Questionnaire

Legislative framework	Assesses the clarity of the incentives policy and its purpose, and the existence of regular reviews and cost assessment and their publicity.
Consultations	Verify the existence of consultations for incentives policy formulation and the communication of changes to the public before they are adopted.
Administration and governance of incentives	Assess the existence of a specific authority awarding incentives, the processes of allocation of incentives, the publicity of their criteria, the notification of investors in case of change to the incentives regime, the publicity of awarded incentives, the existence of justifications for negative decisions and the opportunity to appeal them.
Transparency and access to information	Verify the publication of laws and regulations related to incentives and the existence and publicity of and inventory of incentives, the application process, appeal mechanisms, and statistics about past incentives.

provides for reviews and reforms but not for sharing of information. Lebanon's incentive policy does not have any of these provisions.

Having these provisions in place is one thing and acting upon them is another. Four questions sought to assess whether governments actually (a) carry out regular reviews of the relevance and appropriateness of the incentives policy in pursuing its investment policy objective; (b) carry out regular assessments of the fiscal costs associated with the incentives regime, and (c) whether the review results are published. Of the four countries with reasonably good provisions on paper, two (Morocco and Tunisia) score zero on de facto implementation, while Egypt and Kuwait have some implementation on the ground. Egypt periodically reviews the appropriateness of its incentive regime and makes the results public, but does not assess fiscal costs. Kuwait does both types of assessments but does not make the results public.

Figure 2.19 shows how the scores of the MENA countries progressively decline as one examines existence of an incentive policy, quality of the policy (on paper), and the actual implementation on the ground. Morocco and Tunisia's top position on de jure polices is diluted when de facto implementation is taken into account. Kuwait follows up on policy provisions and carries out assessments of its incentive regime but falls short on transparency. Egypt does not do a comprehensive review but is transparent with what it does. In summary, there appears to be three broad agendas. For one category of countries (Lebanon, Jordan and Oman), getting good de jure policy in place appears to be the immediate agenda. For Morocco, Tunisia and Algeria, it is about ensuring de facto implementation. For Egypt and Kuwait, it is about further deepening the de facto implementation.

FIGURE 2.19

Legislative Framework of Incentive Regimes in MENA, 2015

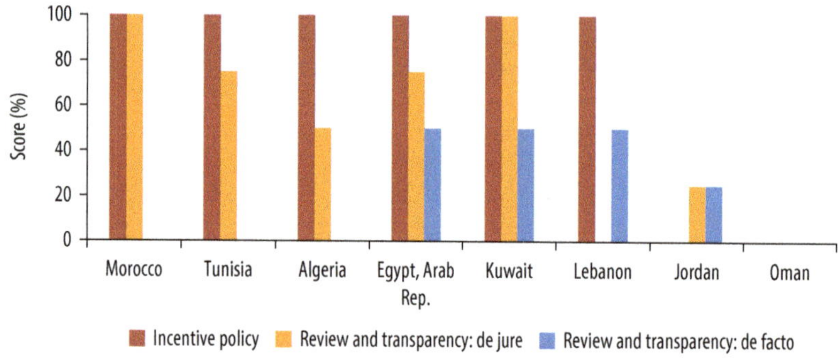

Note: MENA = Middle East and North Africa.

Administration and Governance of Incentives

The administration and governance of incentives influence both the intensity of privilege-seeking behavior and the vulnerability of the system to such influences. Other issues remaining the same, the scope for privileges is likely to increase when multiple agencies are authorized to grant incentives. In six countries, a single authority is in charge of the administration and award of incentives; the exceptions are Lebanon and Algeria, in which such authority is diffused. However, having a single authority is no guarantee that the award of incentives will be immune to privilege-seeking behavior. Three good practice features of the incentive governance regime are important:

- *Rule-based awards.* Award of incentives through a review or screening process, based on a preannounced and published set of criteria.
- *Redress for adverse decisions.* Notification to the investor of specific decisions, with provisions for explaining negative decisions, and for adversely affected investors to appeal to higher authorities.
- *Publication of awards* on incentives awarded.

The performance of the countries on this front is summarized in figure 2.20. Rule-based award of incentives varies widely in the region. Four countries score the maximum possible score: Morocco, Tunisia, Egypt, and Jordan. Algeria and Lebanon score the worst. These scores suggest that half of the countries have some rule-based discipline in the award process. However, in six out of the eight countries, information on incentives awarded is not published. The only exceptions are Algeria

FIGURE 2.20

Governance and Administration of Incentive Regimes in MENA, 2015

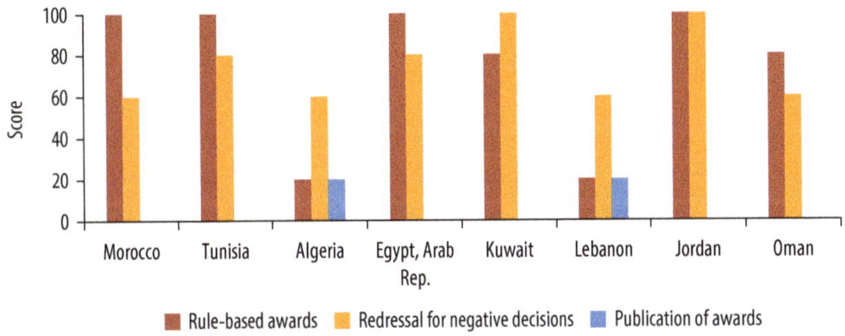

Note: MENA = Middle East and North Africa.

(a paradox, because the country scores poorly on rule-based incentive awards and therefore should have much to hide!) and Lebanon. This suggests that even if a rule-based process exists, as is the case in six countries, there could be scope to manipulate it since the discipline of disclosure is absent. Thus, well-connected businesses will have the incentive and latitude to use their influence and obtain incentives that they do not deserve.

It is interesting to note that all studied countries do relatively better in terms of informing investors about specific decisions and having appeal mechanisms for negative decisions. This is a somewhat paradoxical finding since these governments are not expected to have a strong sense of accountability and provide a grievance redress mechanism for investors. However, it is possible that while an appeals mechanism exists, it may not function to the satisfaction of investors. This aspect was not covered by this study and will require more in-depth work, such as an investor perception survey. This could be part of an analytic agenda following this study.

Transparency and Access to Information

An important aspect of transparency is the publication of laws, regulations, and decrees related to incentives. In countries where the law requires such publication and government complies with the law through actual publication, stakeholders get an opportunity to assess the nature and governance of the incentive regime and raise concerns. They are also in a better position to monitor the administration of the incentives. This introduces some degree of oversight and discipline that may constrain privilege seeking behavior. MENA countries do reasonably well on this front. In six countries, the law provides for such publication, and the governments de facto make these accessible to the public. The exceptions are Kuwait and Oman. In Kuwait, there is no legal requirement for publication; nonetheless, the government does publish the information. The converse is true in Oman, in which the legal requirement to publish is not followed in practice by the government.

While the publication of laws, regulations, and decrees helps enhance transparency, this is further strengthened, and some accountability is achieved, when there is a culture of consultation with stakeholders. Three questions were asked to assess the degree and nature of consultation: (a) whether the law requires consultation during formulation of the laws, regulations, and decrees related to incentives, (b) whether in practice investors are given an opportunity to comment on such documents, and (c) whether any changes to the incentive regime are formally communicated to the public before they are effected.

Figure 2.21 summarizes the findings through the summary data on "consultation." The situation varies widely in the region. In three countries—Egypt, Lebanon, and Morocco—the high degree of transparency in providing information on laws and regulations is combined with a reasonable degree of stakeholder consultation. Stakeholders are informed about the content of the laws and regulations, get some opportunity to comment on the drafting, and are informed about important changes in future. By contrast, in Tunisia, although stakeholders are provided considerable information about laws and regulations once enacted, they do not get an opportunity to comment during the drafting even

FIGURE 2.21

Transparency and Access to Information in MENA, 2015

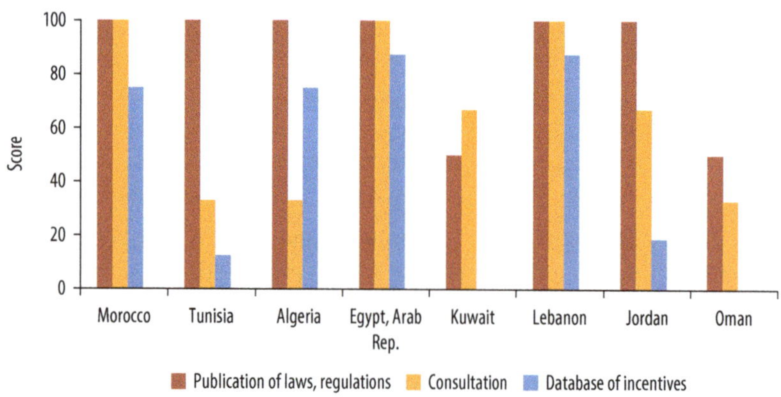

Note: MENA = Middle East and North Africa.

though the law provides for such consultation. In Algeria, they are consulted, but this is not a legal requirement. In neither country are stakeholders informed of any changes in the incentive regime.

A more powerful transparency measure is the existence of an incentives database, for which the MENA countries were assessed on a number of dimensions. These included (a) the existence of a central database or inventory of investment incentives with a comprehensive list of incentives being offered; (b) its accessibility to the public; and (c) the quality of the database in terms of how well it provides information on the nature and administration of the incentive regime and on actual awards of incentives. The country performance varies widely on this measure (see figure 2.20). Whereas Algeria, Egypt, Lebanon, and Morocco have at least two-thirds of the good practice features, Kuwait and Oman have none, and Jordan and Tunisia have very little.

The absence, or poor quality, of the inventory or database on incentives in several MENA countries makes the incentive regimes in these countries particularly vulnerable to privilege seeking. Lack of such data makes under-the-table awards easier to conceal and reduces the ability of any interested body, inside or outside the government, to play a watchdog role.

From the Trees to the Forest: Bringing It All Together

The three categories of good practice features lie on a continuum based on their contribution to making the incentive regime privilege resistant. Having a good policy on incentives, including the provision for review and reassessment, is a beginning. However, more important is the way the incentive regime is governed and administered. Even more important is the degree of transparency of the regime. There is synergy among them. Figure 2.22, which is at a more aggregate level compared to previous figures, summarizes how countries are doing on these three broad categories. On the basis of this, the countries may be divided into the following groups.

Relatively good performers—Egypt and Morocco. These countries do an average job in terms of having a good policy framework on incentives but become progressively better as they move to the administration and governance of the incentive regime, and, finally, to its transparency. This progression is somewhat counterintuitive since developing countries often do better at policy formulation but perform worse as they move to actual administration and governance, and even worse when it comes to transparency and stakeholder engagement. Nonetheless, the lack of a robust policy framework is a matter of concern. Without this, it may be difficult to sustain the good practices currently observed with regard to administration and transparency.

FIGURE 2.22

Privilege Resistance of Investment Incentive Regimes in MENA, 2015

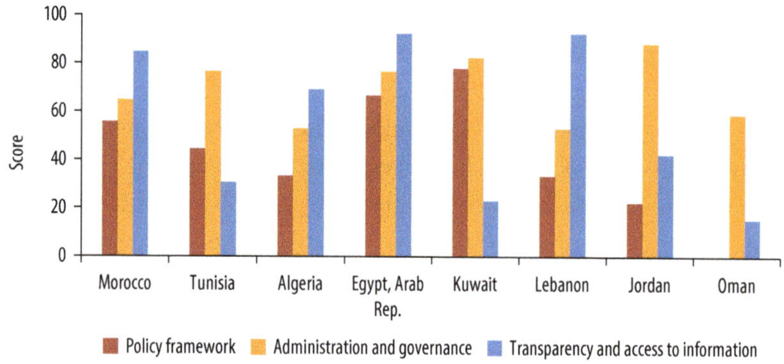

Note: MENA = Middle East and North Africa.

Intermediate performers—Algeria, Kuwait, and Lebanon. Algeria and Lebanon have a similar pattern to that of Egypt and Morocco, except that their performance on policy is much poorer. Weak policy dilutes the robustness of good practices on other fronts. While Algeria's and Lebanon's composite scores on administration and governance is each just a few notches poorer than those of Egypt and Morocco, the two former countries have serious weaknesses. Algeria and Lebanon score very poorly on rule-based award making and publication of information on awards (figure 2.20). These weaknesses make the system particularly vulnerable to privilege seeking.

Kuwait has a different character. While scoring very high on policy and administration, it is very poor on transparency, the second lowest in the sample. In particular, it lacks a database on incentives. This has implications. Even a reasonably good administrative regime for incentives may contain loopholes, and poor transparency may encourage and enable privilege seekers to exploit these, thus undermining the system. While Kuwait scores high on the administration and governance dimension, there is one important area where it is deficient. Kuwait does not publish decisions of positive awards. Thus, it is not easy to know who gets incentives, a weakness further compounded by the lack of a database. This, combined with the general lack of transparency, may make privilege seeking easier.

Poor performers—Tunisia, Jordan, and Oman. Jordan scores the highest in the region on the administration and governance of incentives while the other two countries perform moderately. However, all three countries perform poorly on policy and transparency, with Oman completely lacking an incentive policy. There is synergy between these dimensions of the investment incentive regime. Thus, the relatively better performance of these countries (especially Jordan) on administration and governance may not be a source of comfort because this may be quite vulnerable given the serious weaknesses in other areas.

It appears that the main agenda for Algeria and Lebanon is to have a good policy framework in place, and for Egypt and Morocco to further strengthen the policy framework to consolidate the good practices on other fronts. For Kuwait the main agenda is transparency. For Jordan and Tunisia, it is both policy and transparency. For Oman, improvements are urgently needed across the board. Jordan has already moved towards greater transparency (box 2.2).

BOX 2.2

Jordan: Bringing Transparency to the Incentives Regime

In 2016, with the support of the World Bank, Jordan developed a world-class inventory that is publicly available on the Jordan Investment Commission (JIC)'s e-portal. The inventory is underpinned by an internal information technology (IT) solution administered by a dedicated team. To make the reform sustainable, the government adopted a notification mandating staff to update the inventory annually. This recent reform will now make Jordan one of the top performers for incentives transparency according to the privilege resistance scoring method, s shown in figure B2.2.1.

FIGURE B2.2.1

Transparency and Access to Information on Incentives for MENA Sample Before and After Jordan Inventory Reform
Percent

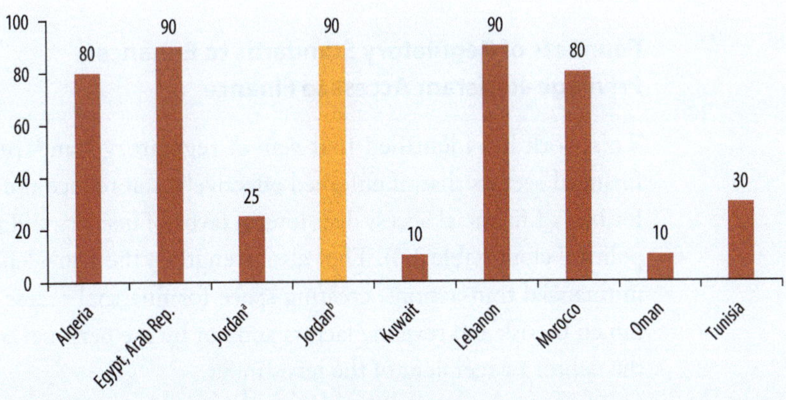

Note: MENA = Middle East and North Africa.
a. Data refer to Jordan before the inventory reform.
b. Data refer to Jordan after the inventory reform.

Access to Finance

Financial systems play a primary role in resource allocation in any modern economy. They act as depositories of household wealth, mobilizing savings and providing the mechanism for channeling this wealth to the different investment choices offered by society. Likened to the circulatory system in human beings, the health of the economy is contingent on ensuring a competitive, efficient, and well-governed financial sector. This contingency is starkly illustrated by the fact that every economic crisis of the past three decades was caused, or accompanied, by a financial crisis compounding the economic and social cost significantly (Litan, Pomerleano, and Sundararajan 2002). A recent success story in terms of improving the transparency of incentives' allocation, in Jordan, is shown in box 2.2.

Financial systems in MENA have not been successful in providing broad access to finance. Surveys show that 39 percent of the region's enterprises considered access to finance to be a major constraint (World Bank 2009). This ratio is very high by international comparison. While MENA's financial sectors are generally large, and the ratio of private credit to gross domestic product (GDP) averages more than 60 percent—with subregional and country variations—only 20 percent of the region's SMEs have a loan or credit. This is a share lower than that in all other middle-income regions. (World Bank 2011)

The nonbank financial systems in MENA are also underdeveloped. Adding this to the banks' restrictive lending practices, enterprises in the region in general and SMEs in particular are left with very few options. The scarcity of capital means that any biases in the allocation decision have a highly distortive effect and are capable of tipping the competitive balance disproportionately.

Four Sets of Regulatory Standards to Enhance Privilege-Resistant Access to Finance

This work has identified four sets of regulatory standards governing financial sectors that, if enforced effectively, can reduce the opportunity for bias of financial access decisions in favor of insiders and persons with political clout (table 2.6). They also strengthen the arm's-length standard in financial transactions, creating space for financial access to be determined by risk and revenue factors and not by the personal connection of the debtor or recipient of the investment.

The most fundamental of these sets of standards focuses on the corporate governance of banks: examining (a) the role of the boards in overseeing high value transactions, (b) the composition of the board, (c) its

TABLE 2.6

Privilege-Resistant Access to Finance Questionnaire

Corporate governance	Verifies that bank boards oversee large loans, have independent administrators, have audit committees chaired by an independent administrator, and receive internal audit reports.
RPT and PEPs	Verifies that the central bank regulates and monitors banks when it comes to related parties and PEPs and that banks have effective mechanisms to deal with related parties and PEPs.
Insider trading	Verifies the existence of rules and sanctions to prevent insider trading that are enforced by an agency through on- and off-site inspections.

Note: PEP = politically exposed person; RPT = related party transactions.

TABLE 2.7

Standards Shielding against Privilege

Privilege-resistant measure	Source of the standard	Original regulatory objective
Corporate governance	Principle 14: Basel Core Principles, Principles for Enhancing Corporate Governance 2010	To provide a degree of confidence essential for the proper functioning of a market economy and prevent difficulties arising from corporate governance shortcomings and affecting the public or the market. Recent revisions were triggered by the financial crisis and specifically geared toward enhancing risk management.
Board oversight over large loans	Principle 19: Concentration Risk and Large Exposure Limits, Basel Core Principles, Principles for Managing Credit Risk 2000	To ensure the safety of the financial institution and its long-term success by maintaining credit risk exposure within acceptable limits.
RPT	Principle 20: Basel Core Principles, Principles for the Management of Credit Risk 200	To ensure the safety of the financial institution and its long-term success by maintaining credit risk exposure within acceptable limits.
Insider trading[a]	Sources including IOSCO's Objectives and Principles of Securities Regulations, Principle 36 on "detecting and deterring manipulation and other unfair practices." International Accounting Standard 24 on Related Parties Disclosures	To promote investors' confidence; protect investors; ensure markets are fair, efficient, and transparent; and reduce systemic risk.
PEPs	Principle 29: Basel Core Principles, FATF Recommendations 2012	To promote high ethical and professional standards and prevent the abuse of the financial system for criminal activities.

Note: FATF = Financial Action Task Force; PEP = politically exposed person; RPT = related party transactions.
a. Falls under the ambit of related parties transaction regulations.

independence, and (d) the audit function. The second and third sets examine the regime regulating related party transactions (RPT) and the standards that guard against the influence of politically exposed persons (PEPs). The fourth set focus on the standards for preventing abuse and biases by insiders.

Each of the four sets of standards combine *regulatory features* that identify what the rules on the books should be to reduce the opportunity for distortion and influence, and *institutional features* that aim to ensure the implementation and enforcement of these rules.

Beyond "Safety and Soundness"

The four sets of regulatory standards that we advocate as potential tools against capture, discretion, and arbitrariness in financial sector capital allocation decisions are derived from a broader set of regulatory standards that are already applicable to the financial sector. With the exception of standards relating to insider trading, ensuring market transparency and efficiency—and the related effective resource allocation function—are not primary objectives of the standards.

This work purports to give these prudential standards explicit market fairness and transparency objectives that improve the resource allocation role of the intermediation process. There is a growing body of research that provides strong basis for this broadening of the use of prudential regulations (World Bank 2013).

Researchers have shown with robust evidence that financial systems have direct impact on growth, and that the main channel for this impact is the role the intermediation system plays in comparing different investment opportunities and allocating capital to the firms with the best potential for growth. Researchers have also demonstrated that the depth of financial markets is just one characteristic of financial systems and is not sufficient to measure the level of financial development. Instead, financial systems are better described in terms of four characteristics: depth, access, efficiency, and stability.

Further evidence has emerged suggesting that the "stability" of financial systems has particularly low correlation with the other attributes. Stable financial systems may be too conservative, providing very low access to finance (that is, failing to fund financially viable projects). The reverse has also been shown to be true. For the purposes of our discussion, it means that applying a prudential standard with only stability in mind may not produce the same result as applying it with the objectives of fairness and effective resource allocation.

Banks' Governance Framework

Reducing the vulnerability of the banking sector to undue influence and distortive practices must start with a strong corporate governance framework. Good corporate governance ensures that decision making is robust, risk is managed transparently and effectively, and rules and standards are adhered to not only in form but in intent throughout the institution.

While there are multiple approaches to good corporate governance, the Basel Committee for Banking Supervision (BCBS) has created a set of principles within which banks and supervisors should operate to ensure that banks are well governed. These include standards for the board's role, composition and practice, senior management, risk management function, and compliance and audit functions.

This work has identified five corporate governance standards that are particularly useful for preventing undue influence and distortion of the banking sector's capital allocation decisions. These standards are (a) board oversight of large loans, (b) board independence, (c) board-level audit committee, (d) independence of the audit committee, and (e) board-level reporting of the audit function. The first two standards are assessed separately in their application to state-owned banks and private banks, thus bringing the total number of variables to seven.

Identifying board oversight over large loans as a key measure in reducing the vulnerability of the banking sector to privilege and undue influence is grounded in well-documented analysis of the performance of the banking sector in MENA. Several studies show that the banking sector, instead of channeling finance to the most productive projects, has allocated large amount of funds to connected businesses, sometimes without enough regard to productivity, ability to repay, or risk management (World Bank 2009, 2011).

The most staggering example of these practices involved loans granted to the family of Ben Ali. Evidence shows that Tunisian banks provided US$1.75 billion (5 percent of all financing by the sector) in funding to businesses linked to the family of President Ben Ali, and nearly 30 percent of the loans were not supported by guarantees of repayment (World Bank 2014b).

The analysis covered two countries: eight MENA and four high-income European countries. Nine of the countries assessed, including five from MENA, scored positively on six or more of the seven indicators measured by this study. Two MENA countries scored positively on four indicators and failed to meet the standard for three out of seven indicators, thus showing a medium level of protection against potential abuse as measured by these criteria. One country out of the sampled 12 adopted just one measure out of the seven identified by this study, thus indicating a very low of resistance to undue influence. Figure 2.23 shows the rate of adoption of each of the identified standards.

FIGURE 2.23

Rates of Adoption of "Privilege Proofing" Corporate Governance Measures in MENA and European Comparators, 2015

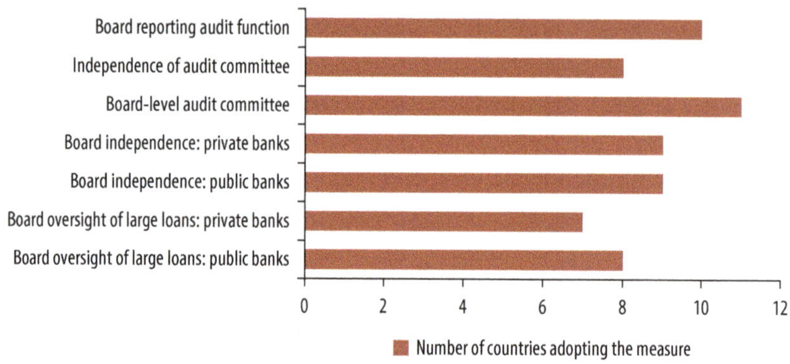

Note: The European comparators are France, Italy, Portugal, and Spain. MENA = Middle East and North Africa.

Public versus Private Banks

MENA is characterized by relatively high level of direct intervention of the state in the supply of banking services in the economy. In 2009, the asset share of government-owned banks in the financial sector stood at 35 percent, higher than all other regions of the world except South Asia. This entrenchment of state-owned banking persists to date, albeit with significant country variations. The set of countries covered by this study can be divided into three categories in terms of the dominance of financial intermediation by state owned banks, as shown in table 2.8 for the entire region.

State banks in MENA are associated with political patronage and the channeling of funds to either unproductive state-owned firms or highly connected private businesses. These practices are typically linked in the literature to inefficiency, weak financial development, low growth, low productivity, less efficiency, and higher rates of nonperforming loans (World Bank 2011, 2013). Therefore, focusing efforts on enhancing governance in public banks and monitoring this indicator separately from an aggregate indicator of good governance become important.

The results of our analysis confirm the trend observed in the above-mentioned literature in one stark way. The one country in the sample that scored the lowest in this set of corporate governance indicators—implementing only one of the measures identified in this taxonomy—is a country with a dominant state-owned banking sector (the asset share of state-owned banks in the financial sector being 86 percent). However, the remaining results are more conflicting. For the two countries that achieved an intermediate score of 4 out of 7 "privilege resistance

TABLE 2.8

State-Owned Bank Shares of Bank Assets in MENA Sample, 2015

State banks dominate intermediation	Algeria,[a] Libya, Syria
Private banks dominate with role of the state significant	Egypt, Arab Rep.[a]; Morocco [a]; Qatar; Tunisia[a]; and United Arab Emirates
Private banks dominate with state role negligible	Bahrain, Jordan[a], Kuwait[a], Lebanon[a], Oman[a], Saudi Arabia, and Yemen, Rep.

Source: Farazi, Feyen and Rocha 2011.
a. Countries for which data are collected for the purposes of this chapter. MENA = Middle East and North Africa.

measures," Egypt has a private-led banking sector with significant share for state-owned banks. In Kuwait, on the other hand, the private sector leads intermediation and the state has a negligible role.

Tunisia and Morocco have significant state ownership in the banking sector yet show a very high score, reflecting near 100 percent adoption of the set of "privilege resistance measures" defined in this work. In Tunisia, scoring 6 out of 7, explaining this finding is more challenging given that evidence from other research has shown that patronage and cronyism have affected the banking sector significantly and that governance reform to address this vulnerability is urgently needed (World Bank 2014b).

Three explanations, borne as well by other research in this area, can be offered to explain these apparent discrepancies. Policy makers should also consider these explanations in interpreting this research and designing any future policy intervention:

- Adopting effective good governance measures in state-owned banks, while difficult and faced with many challenges, is possible and may result in reducing political influence over allocation decisions (World Bank 2013).
- Private sector banks are not immune to the governance issues that plague state banks, and they are vulnerable to political interference, either through lax regulatory environment or privilege capture (World Bank 2009).
- Corporate governance of banks is a very complex issue and often difficult to evaluate externally. Regulatory requirements and pro forma compliance may mask real vulnerability to capture and undue influence (box 2.3).

Arm's-Length Principle

The arm's-length principle is closely linked to the proper functioning of the market. Transactions carried out on market terms should be conducted on

BOX 2.3

Reality Check: Banks' Corporate Governance and Lessons from Crisis

Every financial crisis eventually leads to a conversation about the role of governance in causing the crisis and what can be done about it. Such conversation took place following the Asian financial crisis in 1997. A group of experts made some observations about the complexity of governance in banks (Litan, Pomerleano, and Sundararajan 2002). Some of these observations are important to reflect on here to avoid underestimation of the demands of governance reform even for the narrower purpose of proofing against privilege:

- Bank activities are more opaque; therefore, they are difficult to monitor by shareholders and depositors.
- Bank governance has both public and private dimensions that are mutually reinforcing. Influential financial institutions with poor governance can undermine supervisory governance. The experts noted that the financial sector shows a higher incidence of regulatory capture than other sectors.
- Deposit guarantees create moral hazards that reduce the incentives of management and depositors to monitor good governance.

The 2009 Asian crisis, unlike its predecessors, had its roots in developed financial markets, which made questions about the role of governance even more urgent. With the abundance of investigations of the causes of the crisis, researchers have been able to identify key governance weaknesses that seem to have contributed to the crisis (Kirkpatrick 2009). Again, these findings are useful to contemplate here:

- Firms with better governance averted the worst impact of the crisis.
- Transparency and flow of information through effective channels is a sine qua condition of good governance.
- Some large and well-established banks followed the letter rather than the intent of regulations, adopting a "box ticking" approach to a huge cost. For example, some banks started writing credit lines for 364 days to evade the provisioning requirements triggered by credit terms longer than a year.
- Only 46 percent of audit committee members were very satisfied that their company had an effective process to identify potentially significant business risk, and only 38 percent were very satisfied with the risk reports they received from management (according to a survey of nearly 150 U.K. audit committee members and over 1,000 globally).

an arm's-length basis. The assumption in a market system is that parties to any market transaction are entering such transactions freely and are negotiating to maximize the benefits to themselves. The more such conditions are obtained in the market, the better it functions and the better the market is able to allocate resources rationally across the economy.

Financial markets in this regard are no different. Efforts to protect the markets against the harmful forms of nonarm's-length dealings have resulted in the development of a highly technical area of financial market regulation governing RPT. The emergence of this body of regulations recognizes that RPT occur in the market and aims at ensuring the transparency of these RPT dealings, mandating and enforcing the arm's-length principle, prohibiting the most pernicious forms of RPT, and preventing the potential impact on the stability and soundness of the banking system that may arise from high-risk transactions between related parties.

In the context of the securities market and corporate governance more generally, RPT are regulated with the explicit objective of ensuring market integrity and preserving trust in the market. In the area of banking regulations, regulation of RPT is driven by a concern for the safety and soundness of the banking sector and not directly by concern for the efficient allocation of resources in the economy and the integrity of this allocation mechanism.

This work focuses on the issue of efficient allocation of resources and equality of access to resources, including with respect to access to finance in the banking sector. It does so by looking at RPT regulation not just as a tool for ensuring the safety and soundness of the banking sector but also as an instrument to protect the banking sector against privileged access to capital allocated through the different credit services provided by banks.

To assess the strength of the systems in ensuring an arm's-length standard in the financial market, the research has identified 18 criteria pertinent to assessing the strength of this system in MENA. Thirteen of the criteria relate to lending practices in the banking sector and five relate to trading rules in the securities sector. The criteria relating to lending practices in the banking sector can be grouped into three categories:

- Presence and scope of a regulatory framework that governs RPT with emphasis on transactions with shareholders
- Regulatory framework that determines the standards and governance rules set for implementation of the rules relating to RPT within banks
- Enforcement of the regulatory standards imposed in this area

This is an area of international standardization under the Basel Core Principles and yet the results summarized figure 2.24 reveal very clearly the gap between the adoption of international standards and actual implementation. Although 100 percent of the countries surveyed scored more than 75 percent rate of adoption of regulations governing RPT involving shareholders with adequate scope, this ratio drops to 66 percent when it came to the category of implementation standards required by

TABLE 2.9

Indicators of the Strength of RPT Framework

Scope of regulatory requirement	Implementation standards set by regulations	Enforcement of regulatory standards
• Existence of a regulatory framework governing RPT? • Includes shareholders as individuals? • Includes shareholders as firms? • Includes first-degree relatives? • Includes second-degree relatives?	• Regulations that oblige banks to have policies and procedures to identify exposure to, and transactions with, related parties, including total amount of exposure? • Monitoring and reporting through an independent process? • Policies and procedures that prevent persons benefiting from RPT from taking part in the decision process? • Excludes board members with conflicts of interest from the decision process relating to RPT? • Prior board approvals for all RPT? • Board approval of particularly risky write-offs of related party exposures?	• Monitors through on-site supervision? • Monitors through off-site supervision? • Mechanisms that limit exposures to related parties, such as capital or collateral requirements?

Note: First-degree relatives refer to spouse and children; second-degree relatives refer to other relatives. RPT = related party transactions.

FIGURE 2.24

Strength of Related Party Lending Regulations for All 8 Countries Studied

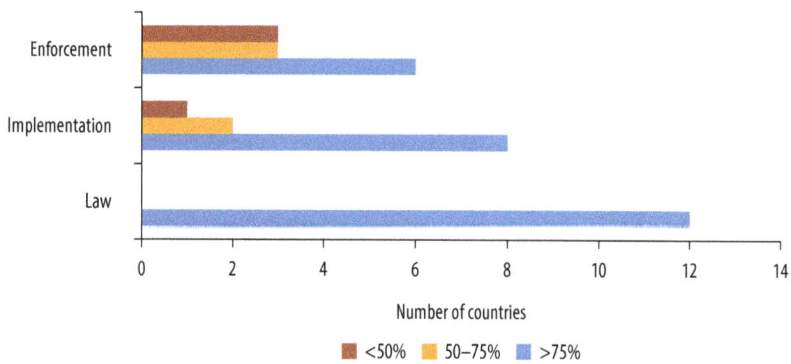

Source: World Bank Competition Policy Team 2015.

regulations, and dropped further to 50 percent for the criteria relating to enforcement of the regulatory standards through inspections and capital adequacy standards.

We now turn to the findings relating to insider trading in the securities market. This is the only dimension of related party trading that the research has dealt with, and it refers to the illegal practice of trading in stock using information obtained through insider access and is not available to the public. The analysis focused on five criteria:

- Rules against insider trading
- Sanctions against insider trading

- Presence of an enforcement agency with jurisdiction over insider trading
- On-site inspection of insider trading regulations
- Off-site inspections of insider trading regulations

The lowest scoring country has one of the smallest stock exchanges in the world, which may explain the less developed framework of insider trading in this country. It is important, however, to place these findings in the broader context of corporate governance and RPT regulation in the region.

In September of 2014, the Organisation of Economic Co-operation and Development (OECD) published the *Guide on Related Party Transactions in the MENA Region*. This guide was based on the results of the survey of 15 Arab Securities Authorities, which was conducted in collaboration with the Union of Arab Securities Authorities (UASA). The report provides findings relating to the regulatory environment of RPT in the corporate nonbanking sector that is worth considering (box 2.4 provides a summary of these findings).

BOX 2.4

RPT in MENA's Corporate Sector

The OECD *Guide on Related Party Transactions in the MENA Region* (2014) identifies a number of trends in RPT in the region and the regulatory frameworks governing them:

- Informality of commercial relations, the prevalence of business groups, holding companies, and ownership concentration create an environment in which RPT can spread.
- The most common RPT in the region are with board members and with companies in the same group. There is also indication that transactions with controlling shareholders are frequent, creating a risk of abuse and weakening minority shareholder protection.
- Another risk of abuse of RPT stems from the common practice in the region of combining a controlling shareholder position with management and key board functions.
- The most common regulatory approach in the region is to allow RPT and mitigate the risks of abuse by imposing review and approval requirements. This approach is also adopted in relation to certain RPT that are typically prohibited by regulators outside the region, such as loans to board members.

(continued on next page)

BOX 2.4

RPT in MENA's Corporate Sector *Continued*

- The most prevalent review mechanism of RPT in the region is ex post review by the shareholders with heavy involvement of the external auditors who are typically required to review and report on RPT (12 jurisdictions require such review). The departure from the common practice globally of relying on the board for review of RPT is consistent with the prevalence of transactions involving board members in the region.
- Global practice indicate that approval mechanisms are most effective when applied ex ante, contrary to MENA practice.
- Common regulatory practice in the region does not adopt a materiality principle, which means all RPT are submitted to the shareholders meeting for ex post approval without selectivity.
- Regulators in the region commonly rely on administrative sanctions and cancellation of illegitimate RPT instead of criminal sanctions.
- Enforcement, however, is a challenge. This is the case across the world. In MENA, it is also affected by the weaknesses in corporate governance regulatory enforcement in general and the capacity of the regulators in this area.
- Reliance on market mechanism instead of being enabled by a robust disclosure system, as is the case in many OECD countries, is not possible because of the nature of the justice system in MENA. Also the nature of the shareholders in the region, including the prevalence of retail investors and the passivity of minority shareholders, renders such mechanisms less effective.
- Information on the incidence of RPT in MENA is generally not publicly available, and it was not reported by the regulators who responded to the survey.

Protecting against Political Clout

The marriage between financial regulation and fighting corruption is now about two decades old. Its roots are in the Abacha case and the efforts of the Nigerian government to recover assets stolen by the Abacha family. This effort led to collaboration with the Swiss authorities and tracing of billions of dollars in Swiss bank accounts, which eventually led to the birth of financial regulations relating to PEPs.

The international standard for regulating financial relationships and transactions involving PEPs is set by the Financial Action Task Force (FATF), which is a standard-setting body on fighting money laundering and combating the financing of terrorism. FATF defines PEPs, in its Forty Recommendations (as amended in 2012), as individuals who are, or have been, entrusted with prominent public functions. The regulatory standards also extend to their family members or close associates. In the 2003 version of the Forty Recommendations, the standard for financial relationships with PEPs was set but restricted to foreign PEPs only, that is, individuals entrusted with such public function in a foreign country. In 2012, the standard was amended and the definition was expanded to extend the measures to domestic PEPs as well as senior officials of international organizations.

The rationale behind regulating financial relationships with PEPs is the recognition that many PEPs have access to public assets and political influence, which offers an opportunity for profiteering and criminal abuse, such as bribery and corruption. The objective of the measures is to ensure that financial institutions are not misused by PEPs to hide the proceeds of crime and to evade law enforcement.

It is important to have some basic idea about what anti–money-laundering measures relating to PEPs do. These measures require financial institutions entering into relationships with customers to exercise customer due diligence and to have mechanisms in place to identify customers who are politically exposed, including their family members and close associates. Historically, and until 2012, the international standard was concerned only with foreign PEPs, driven by concerns about money laundering. It was recognized that foreign PEPs pose higher risk of abusing the financial system to launder their money. They were also less known to the local financial institutions, which were interpreted as presenting a higher degree of risk.

In 2012, the system of prevention was extended to domestic PEPs as well, but some distinction between the two categories persist. Once a customer is identified as a foreign PEP, enhanced due diligence measures are immediately triggered. In the case of domestic PEPs, mere identification as a domestic PEP does not automatically trigger enhanced due diligence. Instead, financial institutions are required to assess the risk and determine whether the relationship poses high risk based on other risk factors to be determined by the institution.

Like the previous standards discussed in this document, the original objective of this framework of regulatory standards is not to prevent privileged access to the resources allocated by the financial system itself. Instead, this system is designed to help tackle the issue of corruption more broadly by providing another instrument for detection and law enforcement.

In this study, data were gathered to assess the strength of the sampled countries in fighting the abuse of the financial system by PEPs. Four criteria were examined: (a) whether there is a system regulating relationships with PEPs; (b) whether this system sets enhanced due diligence rules for financial relationships with PEPs, (c) whether this system sets recordkeeping rules for such relationships; and (d) whether the regulatory authorities audit banks for compliance with these rules.

The results confirm a gap between having a law on the books regulating an activity and actual implementation and enforcement of the rule. As figure 2.25 shows, while only one of the MENA countries examined does not have a rule regulating financial sector relationships with PEPs, six out of the eight countries examined do not have regulatory enforcement of the applicable rules in this area.

In addition, only two of the seven countries that have rules on the books regulating PEPs engagement with the financial sector apply these rules only to foreign PEPs and exclude domestic PEPs. This issue of scope is particularly relevant to this study, which looks to the rules regulating financial sector services to PEPs as one instrument in proofing the economic system against privilege. So in reality only two countries out of the eight examined actually deploy anti–money-laundering preventive measures in the fight against domestic corruption.

This is the only regulatory area examined in this chapter in which there is a big gap between the strength of the regulatory system in sampled MENA countries as compared to the strength of the same system in sampled southern European countries. While three out of the four southern European countries examined satisfy all four criteria of strength tested in this work, only one of the eight MENA countries examined achieve this result; four satisfy less than 25 percent of the criteria and three satisfy 50 percent.

FIGURE 2.25

Privilege-Resistance of PEP Regulations in MENA, 2015

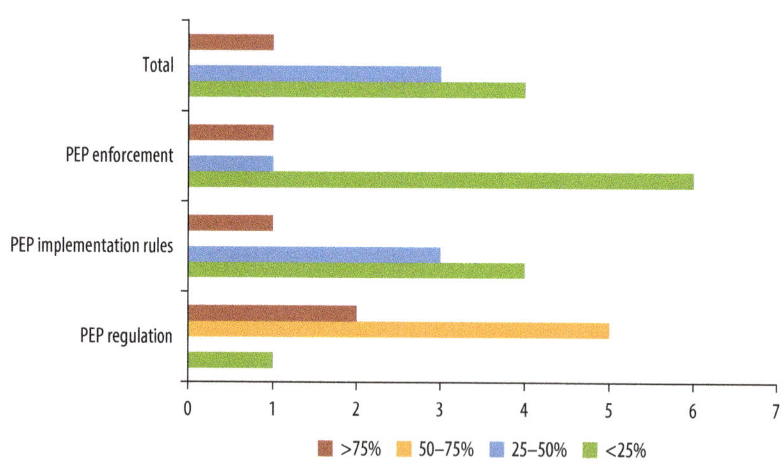

Note: MENA = Middle East and North Africa; PEP = politically exposed persons.

FIGURE 2.26

Strength of PEP Regulations in Southern Europe Comparators, 2015

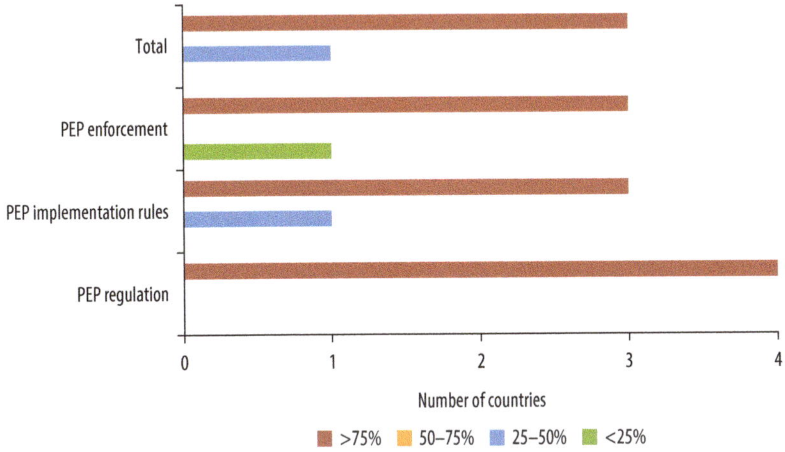

Note: PEP = politically exposed persons.

Beyond the law, implementation matters

There is a clear gap between the law on the books and rules of implementation and actual enforcement. This gap will need to be addressed if the areas of regulation examined in this work are to be effectively deployed as instruments against privilege capture in the financial sector. Improving performance against the indicators in this study will be directly affected by the strength of the overall supervisory capacity in the financial sector as well as by standards and practice of corporate governance in the sector.

Unleashing the ability of these regulatory measures to make the financial sector resistant to privileged access will also require stretching the logic of these regulatory standards beyond mere financial market stability, safety, and soundness and toward market integrity, access, and inclusion as regulatory objectives.

Competition Policy

Market competition is a key driver for achieving greater innovation, productivity, and economic growth. Greater competition is enabled through a comprehensive competition policy framework that includes a set of policies and laws ensuring competition in the marketplace is not restricted in such a way as to reduce economic welfare (Motta 2004). In practical terms, competition policy involves two pillars: (a) the promotion of measures to enable contestability, firm entry, and rivalry; and (b) the enforcement of antitrust laws (typically rules against abuse of dominance and anticompetitive agreements, and merger control) and state aid control (table 2.10).[7] The former involves the improvement of regulations and administrative procedures by government bodies, while the latter focuses on business behavior of all entities that perform commercial functions. The ultimate aim of competition policies is not to increase the number of firms in a market or to eliminate market power to achieve a theoretical state of perfect competition. Instead, the final goal is to generate the right incentives for firms to improve their economic performance in terms of their actual and potential rivals and in so doing deliver the best outcomes for consumers and the economy as a whole.

The available competition policy tools and the extent to which competition policies are implemented vary across countries. Since the competitive environment in any country will be affected by government interventions,[8] policies, and regulations, there is scope to implement pillar 1 on procompetition market regulation[9] to varying degrees in any country. Pillar 2 (competition enforcement), on the other hand, usually requires a competition law to be enacted and a competition authority (or other responsible body) to enforce the law. Thus, for countries without a competition law or an operational competition authority, the focus of competition policy will lie in pillar 1 in the short- to medium-term.

Pillar 1, which consists of procompetition regulations and government interventions, comprises (a) regulation of network sectors to simulate

TABLE 2.10

Comprehensive Competition Policy Frameworks

Pillar 1: procompetition regulations and government interventions (for example, opening markets and removing anticompetition sectoral regulation)	Pillar 2: effective competition rules and antitrust enforcement
Reform policies and regulations that strengthen dominance (for example, restrictions to the number of firms, statutory monopolies, bans toward private investment, lack of access regulation for essential facilities)	Tackle cartel agreements that raise the costs of key inputs and final products and reduce access to a broader variety of products
Eliminate government interventions that are conducive to collusive outcomes or increase the costs of competing (for example, controls on prices and other market variables that increase business risk)	Prevent anticompetitive mergers
Reform government interventions that discriminate and harm competition on the merits (for example, frameworks that distort the level playing field or grant high levels of discretion)	Strengthen the general antitrust framework to combat anticompetitive conduct and abuse of dominance
	Control state aid to avoid favoritism, ensure competitive neutrality, and minimize distortions on competition[a]

Source: Adapted from Kitzmuller and Licetti 2012.
a. This subtopic is included under pillar 2 since it comprises economywide rules. However, it could be considered to be a separate pillar since it is often developed outside of rules on anticompetitive behavior of firms and merger control.

competitive market outcomes; (b) infusing competition principles in different public policies (for example, public procurement, trade, investment, and industrial policies); and (c) conducting competition assessments in regulatory impact assessments of procedures, regulations, or policies to understand their impact on competition and to identify more procompetitive alternatives.

When a competition law has been enacted and a functional competition authority is in place, competition enforcement (pillar 2) complements economic market regulation (pillar 1). Competition authorities monitor and punish anticompetitive behavior by firms and prevent mergers that could harm competition. Competition authorities typically support pillar 1 with advocacy efforts, conducting research on the effect on competition of proposed government interventions, and providing opinions on their unintended impacts on market functioning and potential alternatives to minimize market distortions. In some cases, a new competition authority may find it more effective to focus on these advocacy efforts in the early stages of its development while it develops its enforcement capacity.

Interacting competition policy with other policies and introducing competition principles can make those broader policies more effective. There is evidence that the introduction of market-based competitive voucher schemes into subsidy programs has positive effects. Industrial policy can also benefit from being complemented by competition policy. Other studies find that sectoral industrial policies (such as subsidies or tax holidays) have a larger impact on productivity growth when targeted at competitive sectors or when they are allocated in such a way as to preserve or increase competition (for example, by inducing entry or encouraging younger enterprises). Trade policy is another key tool policy makers can use to enhance competition and welfare in the absence of a competition enforcement framework. Finally, competition law enforcement (pillar 2) can complement traditional poverty reduction measures such as direct cash transfers to the poor from the State (World Bank and OECD, 2017).

Objective and Methodological Approaches

This chapter focuses only on the competition law aspects that ensure a system of checks and balances and that reduce the risks of undue private and public influence over the competition policy and decision-making process. The analysis is mainly based upon a review of the competition laws of Algeria, Morocco, Tunisia, Egypt, Kuwait, Oman, Lebanon, and Jordan (hereinafter, "the studied MENA countries"). In terms of methods, it builds upon the Markets and Competition Policy Assessment

TABLE 2.11

Competition Law and Policy Questions and Rationale

Questions	Rationale based on potential outcomes
Effective enforcement of competition law	
• Is there a competition law in place? Does the competition legal framework include provisions that address horizontal and vertical agreements, abuse of dominance, merger control, anticompetitive regulation or competition advocacy, or actions of public officials that facilitate anticompetitive behavior?	• Weak competition legal framework limits the ability to tackle anticompetitive behavior and anticompetitive regulation
• Are there economic sectors or enterprises exempted from the application of the competition framework (for example, SOEs, state bodies or agencies, professional associations)?	• Exceptions may create/enhance privileges for economic sectors or enterprises
• Is there a specific framework and procedure that public bodies should follow to grant state aid (subsidies, tax breaks, government land, concessional loans) to private enterprises and SOEs in such a way to minimize competition distortions?	• Lack of transparency may result in discretion, arbitrariness, and privileges for few
• Is there a functional competition authority in place (that is, with executive regulations in place to implement the law, and endowed with staff and a budget)?	• Weak enforcement capacity can limit the ability to tackle anticompetitive behavior and anticompetitive regulations
• Does the competition authority have the mandate to issue opinions on government policies and draft legislation and regulations as part of its role in advocacy? Are the opinions binding or is there a mechanism to monitor their implementation?	• Weak competition advocacy may limit the ability of the competition authority to identify and seek the removal of anticompetitive regulation, with potential for protecting certain interests
• Does the competition authority have the necessary power and tools to uncover illegal practices (for example, case prioritization, adequate fines, leniency program, inspection powers)?	• Weak enforcement capacity may limit the ability to tackle anticompetitive behavior of private and public operators
Maintaining trust and independence in competition law and policy implementation	
• Is the competition authority entrusted with enforcing competition an independent body or a ministerial department?	• Weak competition framework may result in using the competition authority for goals that are alien to competition
• Is the competition authority accountable before the legislative or executive powers?	• Lack of accountability may result in discretion and arbitrariness in implementation
• Can an anticompetitive merger or acquisition be allowed on grounds other than competition (for example, public interest)?	• Noncompetition criteria may result in discretion, arbitrariness, and privileges for few
• Is there an objective procedure to select and dismiss the board members of the competition agency?	• Lack of transparency may result in undue political pressure on the competition authority
• To ensure continuity in operations and strategy implementation, are board members jointly nominated or at intervals?	• The joint nomination of board members may affect institutional stability and reduce the incentives to act independently
• May the competition authority's board members hold other offices or appointments in the government or the industry?	• The possibility to hold incompatible appointments in the public and private sectors reduces incentives to act independently
• Is there a cooling-off period during which board members and staff of the competition authority cannot take jobs in the government or companies investigated after their term of office/employment contract?	• The absence of a cooling-off period reduces incentives to act independently
• Are there different teams from the competition authority/(ies) involved in opening the investigation, prosecuting, and reaching a decision?	• Lack of internal mechanisms of checks and balances increases discretion and may result in discretion, arbitrariness, and privileges for the few
• Are there rules to avoid conflicts of interest of case handlers and members of the decision body?	• Lack of conflicts of interest rules reduces incentives to act independently
• What is the financing mechanism of the competition authority?	• The lack of financial autonomy of the competition agency reduces incentives to act independently

(continued on next page)

TABLE 2.11

Competition Law and Policy Questions and Rationale *Continued*

Questions	Rationale based on potential outcomes
Procedural fairness and transparency	
• Can the competition authority's decisions be vetoed by the line ministry(ies) or any other body of the executive branch?	• Lack of transparency and discriminatory enforcement may result in privileges for the few
• Are there protections for ensuring that confidential or privileged business information provided by companies during investigations, merger reviews, and market studies is not disclosed to third parties?	• Technical weakness may be used by business parties and third parties and may result in discretion, arbitrariness, and privileges for the few
• Are the competition authority's decisions subject to effective review by an independent appellate body?	• Lack of judicial control may result in discretion, arbitrariness, and privileges for the few

Note: SOE = state-owned enterprise.

Toolkit developed by the Trade and Competitiveness Global Practice Competition Policy Cluster and the OECD good governance framework for regulators.[10] In addition, it draws upon a framework of good principles for market and competition authorities, elaborated by Ottow (2015).

Our analysis includes three main aspects that should be enacted so competition authorities can avoid undue public or private influence in the implementation of competition laws:

- Effective enforcement of the competition law, including a subsidy or state aid control framework
- Maintain trust in and independence of the competition authorities
- Procedural fairness and transparency of the competition authorities' activities (see also table 2.12)

These three areas were embedded in a questionnaire on competition law and policy that was answered by competition authorities and local experts in the selected MENA countries during 2015. The questions were selected to identify elements that may result in a higher risk of public or private influence on competition law implementation because they (a) weaken the competition legal framework or its effective enforcement; (b) reduce the ability and incentives of competition authorities (board members or staff) to act independently; or (c) increase the room for discretion in competition law implementation that may result in shielding a limited number of enterprises or economic sectors from competition (see appendix A, tables A.1, A.2, and A.3, which provide examples of competition law and policy questions and rationale).

Competition authorities may be exposed to risks of undue influence by both private and public parties. Undue private sector influence may be associated with formal and informal barriers to entry embedded in public policies that confer competition privileges to a few (often unproductive)

TABLE 2.12

Implementing the Competition Policy and Legal Framework

Legal and policy framework	Operational framework	Enforcement of competition law	Creation of competition culture
Competition policy	Functioning rules and structure of agency	Competition regulations (bylaws)	Awareness raising for private sector, civil society, journalists, academia, public sector
Competition law	Staffing and financial resources for the agency	Capacity building for staff and board members	Capacity building for stakeholders
Other relevant laws • Framework for regulation of trade • Sectoral legal frameworks • Public procurement law • Public service legal framework • State aid control framework	Operating manual, staff code of conduct	nonbinding guidelines for enforcement	Collaboration with regulators and ministries within the government
	Strategy for operationalizing the law: priorities, milestones	Internal procedural guidelines	Opinions on relevant laws / regulations that might likely harm competition
	M&E and impact evaluation framework	Case handling (anticompetitive practices and merger review)	Market studies in sectors with competition concerns

Source: World Bank 2016c.
Note: M&E = monitoring and evaluation.

incumbents. As a consequence, the latter may gain a competitive edge because of their connections or their ability to influence policy making and delivery, including competition policy implementation. On the other hand, public capture covers those situations in which the competition institutional setup does not provide for sufficient safeguards against political pressures, cronyism, and interference with their core mandate of competition authorities to protect competition and consumer welfare (World Bank 2016c).

This chapter constitutes only one entry point toward a more in-depth review of those competition policy aspects that may give rise to undue private and public influence in the selected MENA countries. Its scope reflects a desk review of the competition laws of the selected MENA countries. Hence, a more detailed analysis will be required to provide a complete assessment of key issues, especially in relation to procedural fairness, agency architecture or funding mechanisms, as well as a review of competition issues that are affecting specific sectors of those economies.

Competition Legal Framework

The number of jurisdictions with competition laws has almost tripled in 15 years in Africa. In 2000, 13 jurisdictions had adopted competition laws (12 countries and one regional bloc). By 2015, this number had increased to 32 jurisdictions (27 countries and 5 regional blocs). Competition authorities have been operating in 22 countries and two regional communities for an average of 10 years. Competition authorities start operating four years, on average, after the law is passed, but in some cases there has been a considerable delay. In the African region, Algeria and Cameroon, for example, established their competition authorities 18 and 10 years, respectively, after the laws providing for their establishment were passed. Madagascar and the Central African Economic and Monetary Community (CEMAC) have not yet operationalized the framework after more than 10 and 16 years, respectively. Tunisia's Competition Council, in operation since 1992, is one of the oldest competition authorities in Africa; the Monopolies and Prices Department under Kenya's National Treasury began implementing an early version of that country's competition law in 1989 (World Bank and ACF 2016).

An effective competition law applies across all sectors of the economy and to all economic agents, be they public or private, and provides an institutional setup to enforce the competition law. Although this is the typical situation in the selected European Union countries,[11] it is not always the case in the selected MENA countries. In the MENA region, some countries do not have a competition law (Lebanon) or a fully staffed competition agency and procedural framework to develop its activities (Kuwait), or have not investigated competition cases so far despite having a competition law and an agency in place (Oman) (table 2.13). Three out of seven countries with a competition law have recently amended it (Kuwait is currently in the process of finalizing the adoption of a new competition law), and three out of seven countries have had a competition authority for 10 years or more.

Exceptions to the competition law unrelated to efficiency reasons are common in the selected MENA countries. These may limit the effectiveness of the competition law and may reinforce distortions in the market. From the seven MENA countries with a competition law, six provide

TABLE 2.13

Competition Laws and Competition Authorities in MENA, 2015

Country	Year of enactment of current competition law[a]	Year in which authority started operations based on previous version of the competition law
Algeria	2003	2013
Egypt, Arab Rep.	2014	2006
Jordan	2004	2002
Kuwait	2007	Not operational yet
Morocco	2014	2009
Oman	2014	2011
Tunisia	2015	1992

Source: World Bank Competition Policy Team 2015.
a. The oldest competition law is taken into consideration.

FIGURE 2.27

Sectors and Economic Agents Excluded from Competition Legal Frameworks in MENA, 2015

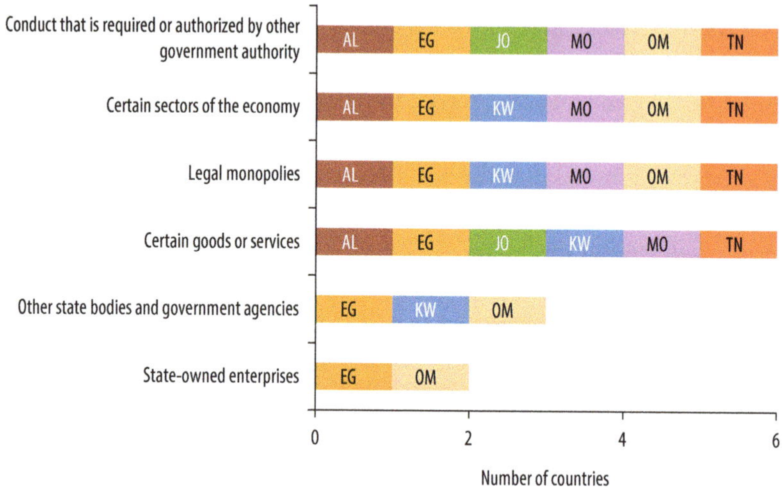

Source: World Bank Competition Policy Team 2015.
Note: AL = Algeria; EG = Egypt, Arab Rep.; JO = Jordan; KW = Kuwait; MENA = Middle East and North Africa; MO = Morocco; OM = Oman; TN = Tunisia.

for certain exceptions at the sector or type of economic agents levels (see figure 2.27):

- In Tunisia, there is an exclusion of sectors or areas in which competition is limited by virtue of a monopoly and first necessity goods or services, or goods and services facing durable difficulties of supply.
- In Morocco, competition law excludes professional associations, regulated sectors, and sectors with a legal monopoly or where state aid is potentially granted.
- SOEs are excluded from the scope of the competition law in Egypt and Oman. There is a lack of clarity regarding the scope of exceptions for SOEs in Kuwait; the law does not apply to public projects and facilities managed directly by the state (for example, the competition law does not apply to the oil sector).
- The competition authority may decide to exclude the application of the competition law on a case by case basis in Algeria and Egypt.

In most MENA countries in the sample, the scope of the competition laws is consistent with typical substantive provisions. Competition laws have a broad scope of application, addressing all forms of anticompetitive conduct (horizontal and vertical agreements, abuse of dominance) and anticompetitive mergers. This is the overall approach in the selected

FIGURE 2.28

Scope of Competition Laws in MENA, 2015

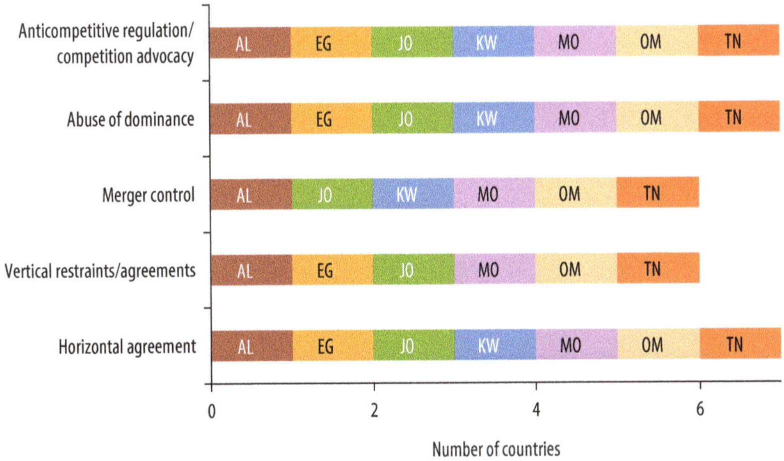

Source: World Bank Competition Policy Team 2015.
Note: AL = Algeria; EG = Egypt, Arab Rep.; JO = Jordan; KW = Kuwait; MO = Morocco; OM = Oman; TN = Tunisia.

MENA countries that have a competition law in place with few exceptions (notably, merger control in Egypt[12]) (figure 2.28).

However, the definition of market dominance needs to be improved in most of the MENA countries. In relation to determining market dominance and anticompetitive practices, good practice recommends a "market effects–based" approach, which considers countervailing economic efficiencies (with the exception of hardcore cartels) and does not establish market dominance on the basis of market shares. While this is the standard approach in the European Union countries, several of the selected MENA countries establish market dominance based on market shares (Kuwait—35 percent, Oman—35 percent, Jordan—40 percent), which may negatively affect the ability of firms with market power to compete on the merits.

Most of the selected MENA competition authorities have a general mandate to carry out advocacy activities, but few can act against anticompetitive regulation. An effective competition law provides the basis for a strong advocacy role of competition agencies to promote competition principles in other policies. In the case of European Union, the competition legal framework is also complemented by a state aid and subsidy control legal framework to minimize competition distortions in the markets. According to the competition laws in the selected MENA countries, the competition advocacy role should be the responsability of the MENA competition authorities as in the European Union countries. However, more important than having an explicit advocacy mandate is the way in which it is implemented. In this regard, only the competition law of Morocco provides the competition authority with the tools to monitor the implementation of their competition opinions on draft laws and existing legislation.[13]

With regard to the ability to conduct market inquiries and studies, all MENA competition authorities have this power by law. The competition authorities from Jordan,[14] Morocco,[15] and Egypt[16] indicated they carried out several sector inquiries in 2013–14 (see figure 2.29).

Subsidy and state aid control regimes are not present in the selected MENA countries as opposed to the European Union ones. Beneficiaries that receive subsidies and state aid or other state support measure enjoy a comparative advantage over their competitors that is not necessarily associated with their efficiency. Control of subsidies and state support measures is a necessary safeguard for effective competition, free trade, and efficient management of fiscal resources. In the European Union, where state aid originated, it can be defined as any form of public assistance extended to an undertaking by public authorities on a selective basis. State aid encompasses a wide range of state support including direct subsidies, tax concessions, state guarantees, and investments from public funds in circumstances in which a private investor would not have invested. The Treaty for the Functioning of the European Union generally prohibits state aid unless it is justified by reasons of general economic development. Although state aid is a typically European concept, a few African jurisdictions have included provisions on state aid control in their acts (The Seychelles, Togo, and the East African Community) (World Bank and ACF 2016).

Most of the MENA countries lack enforcement powers to effectively deter anticompetitive behavior. In addition to a clear and complete legal mandate, competition enforcers (competition authorities) typically have the powers and tools necessary to enforce the competition law. Typically, these powers include instruments, such as adequate fines, leniency programs to foster cartel detection,[17] powers to request information from the companies (summons or subpoena) and to conduct surprise inspections (dawn raids), powers to seize documents, and ability to reach settlements with parties involved in anticompetitive behavior that cooperate with the competition authority. This is the case in the selected European Union countries. In contrast, several MENA competition authorities lack fully fledged enforcement powers, which can reduce the probability of detection of most harmful anticompetitive practices (such as hardcore cartels) and can hinder the effectiveness of leniency policies.

Moreover, certain MENA countries have adopted a prosecutorial model, in which the agency simply brings enforcement actions against those who violate the law. This fails to provide the necessary tools for agencies to function in a complex and dynamic business environment (figure 2.29). For instance, Kuwait, Oman, Algeria, Jordan do not have leniency programs,[18] although the leniency programs can be effective in detecting and proving the existence of cartels because they allow a cartel member to confess to its involvement in a cartel and cooperate fully with a cartel investigation by providing evidence that will aid in proceedings against another cartel member. The power to settle violations is scant, the exceptions being Egypt, Tunisia, Morocco. Certain countries rely on a prosecutorial model by which the competition authority simply brings enforcement actions against those who violate the law to the courts (Egypt[19]) or refer the case to the public prosecutor (Jordan and Oman).

Large fines can be a significant deterrent against cartel activity, but fines imposed in the selected MENA countries are relatively low (based on information submitted in the questionnaire). In most jurisdictions, the fines for hardcore cartels and anticompetitive practices, as stated in the law, are below the levels encountered in international practice (10 percent of turnover). For example, fines are below 10 percent of the annual turnover in Jordan and Algeria as shown in figure 2.29. In terms of enforcement, Egypt emerges as an outlier in the MENA region with fines totaling US$2.6 million in 2014 and a record fine of US$25.5 million imposed to the largest steel manufacturer for abusing its

FIGURE 2.29

Powers of the Competition Authorities in MENA, 2015

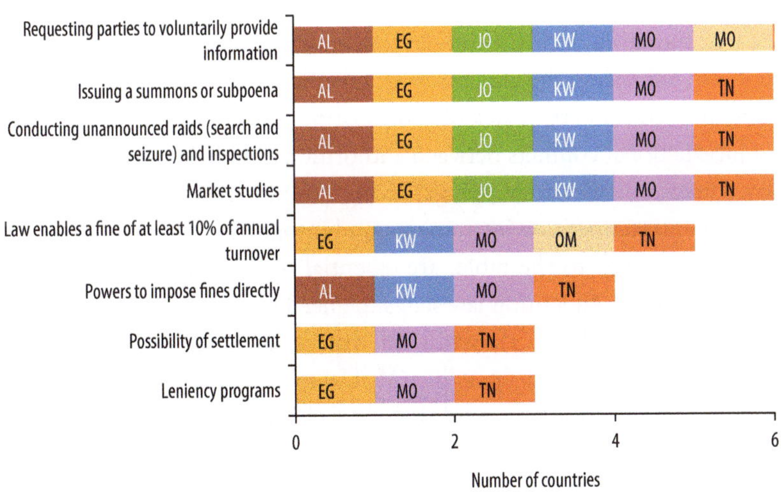

Source: World Bank Competition Policy Team 2015.
Note: AL = Algeria; EG = Egypt, Arab Rep.; JO = Jordan; KW = Kuwait; MENA = Middle East and North Africa; MO = Morocco; OM = Oman; TN = Tunisia.

dominant position in the steel market during 2005–06. Besides Egypt, only Tunisia, with its Tunisian Competition Council, indicated the imposition of fines for breach of the competition rules (around US$614,000 in 2013; US$103,000 in 2014). The imposed fines for the competition law infringement seems to be low. As shown by Ivaldi, Jenny, and Khimich (2016), even in the case of a country with an established enforcement record, such as South Africa, fines are only 9 percent of the excess profits, on average considering four cases, compared to 26 percent in the European Union.[20]

Furthermore, competition authorities in MENA are assigned conflicting goals, such as regulating prices. In contrast with standard practice of competition laws in the selected European Union countries, the MENA countries' competition laws may include conflicting goals, including the opportunity to introduce price controls.[21] Price control rules are among the regulatory tools instituted by governments, often with the aim of protecting consumers from excessively high prices or protecting the incomes of small producers. While regulating prices in traditional monopoly sectors (for example, natural monopolies in utilities) or as a response to supply shocks might be warranted, competition authorities that impose price controls in markets with many potential suppliers may have adverse effects. In fact, price regulation can act as a barrier to competition by, for example, distorting incentives for entry and investment and innovation, or distorting the dynamics of price-based competition by preventing firms from putting downward pressures on prices. To that end, the European Union countries' competition agencies have steered away from such conflicting goals[22] and have concluded protocols of collaboration with other regulators to prevent situations of conflict.[23]

Collaboration between competition authorities and sector regulators is key to enhancing the effectiveness and efficiency of their actions to the benefit of consumers. A lack of coordination may generate risks in terms of jurisdictional conflicts between authorities, double jeopardy for regulated firms, and forum shopping. Having a common understanding of the market and competition instruments, and recognizing the value that each authority brings to the table, are essential for collaboration. In some countries, the competition law states the need for collaboration (Algeria, Morocco, and Tunisia), while in others authorities have signed Memorandums of Understanding (MoUs) to encourage greater collaboration. However, in the case of the selected MENA countries, there are few protocols signed with regulators (Oman, Algeria—no protocols signed; Jordan and Tunisia—only with the telecom regulator, Kuwait—only with the Statistics Agency).[24]

Maintaining Trust and Independence in Competition Policy Implementation

In some cases, the independence of decision making may be affected by the current legal framework in the selected MENA countries. Drawing on international best practices, it is possible to identify a series of entry points that help prevent undue external influence from the private and public actors. A key aspect of the independence of a competition authority is the ability to act without day-to-day management of a minister or the political bodies of government. This includes the power to make final decisions with direct effect on firms that engaged in anticompetitive behavior. Only a high degree of independence helps insulate the authorities from political pressures, cronyism, and interference with their core mandate to safeguard competition. Technical independence may be compromised in cases that: (a) a competition authority is a department in a line ministry, (b) a line ministry can revoke, has veto powers, or has the final saying on decisions and cases, (c) the line ministry is responsible for industry matters, which might conflict with the pursuit of purely competition goals.

In the selected MENA countries, the independence of the competition agency decisions may be affected by the absence of full institutional independence under the existing legal framework (figure 2.30). In the selected MENA countries, competition policy is entrusted as follows. Authorities with administrative and financial autonomy, reporting to a line ministry include Oman, Algeria, Morocco, Tunisia, Egypt, Kuwait. In Jordan, the competition body is a ministry directorate. The line ministers are the Minister of Commerce and Industry (Kuwait and Oman),

FIGURE 2.30

Status of Competition Authorities in MENA, 2015

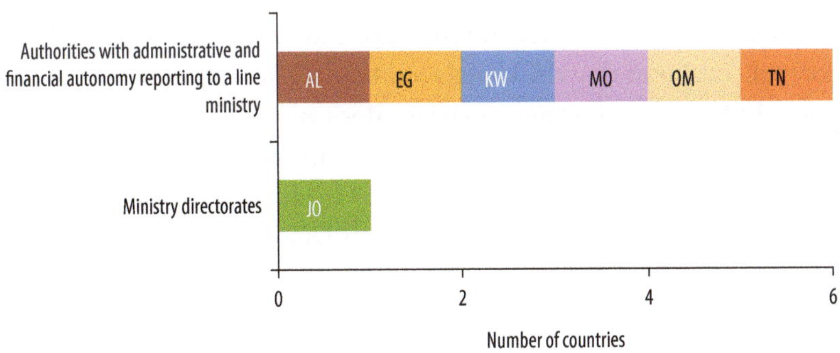

Source: World Bank Competition Policy Team 2015.

Note: AL = Algeria; EG = Egypt, Arab Rep.; JO = Jordan; KW = Kuwait; MENA = Middle East and North Africa; MO = Morocco; OM = Oman; TN = Tunisia.

the Ministry of Commerce (Algeria), the Ministry of Industry and Trade (Jordan), the Ministry of General Affairs and Governance (Morocco), the Ministry of Commerce (Tunisia), and the Cabinet of Ministers (Egypt).

Out of the six selected MENA countries with a merger control regime in place, two allow their governments to reverse a prohibited merger (Algeria and Morocco), while one (Tunisia) gives the line minister the competence to assess if the concentration is illegal. Moreover, competition authorities can consider other public interests when authorizing a merger (for example, Tunisia, Morocco, Jordan, Kuwait—the competition law does not specify the economic test for allowing or prohibiting a merger), which normally leads to a more restrictive assessment of mergers than in a scenario in which a methodology based exclusively on competition considerations is followed. In addition, competition authorities must set clear boundaries and criteria for the application of a public interest test. For example, South Africa requires that a public interest consideration be merger-specific and substantial. Botswana, Kenya, Zambia, and South Africa are some of the countries that have or are in the course of drafting guidelines on the assessment of public interest considerations. Contrary to the aforementioned examples, the selected MENA countries with a public interest test have not issued guidelines to facilitate implementation and increase predictability: Kuwait does not define the grounds for allowing or prohibiting a merger in the competition law; Tunisia adopts a broad objective of technical or economic progress but adds that national consolidation and the competitiveness of national companies at the international level will also be taken into account; Algeria merely refers to public interest considerations; Morocco lists employment, international competitiveness of domestic firms, and industrial development; while Jordan mentions employment, encouraging exports, attracting investment, and the ability of domestic companies to compete internationally.

Heads of governments and ministries in MENA appear to play a key role in appointing the board members of the competition authorities, but the appointment process does not follow best practice. Good practice suggests that the appointment of competition authority board members should be made at intervals and based on objective criteria. This is the case of the selected European Union countries with board members appointed by national parliaments at intervals following objective criteria and with dismissal limited to specific situations.

According to the replies to the Competition Law and Policy Questionnaire, in the selected MENA countries, board members are appointed by governments (or the king in Morocco, sultan in Oman, or president in Algeria), but not always at intervals and in accordance with objective appointment and dismissal rules. Only Jordan provided for the possibility of nominating board members at intervals. Oman and Jordan have no rules in terms of mandates' duration. Oman, Algeria, and Kuwait lack objective dismissal rules. Box 2.5 cites the privilege-resistant characteristics to include in the institutional design of a competition authority.

BOX 2.5

Institutional Design Models

It is widely recognized that competition authorities require a substantial degree of independence to conduct their activities in a professional, technical, nonpartisan, competent, and effective manner. According to a 2015 World Bank/African Competition Forum (ACF) survey, most agencies responsible for the administration of competition policy in Africa are structured as independent bodies. Out of 28 authorities surveyed, 64 percent identify themselves as structurally independent bodies. Under at least 10 regimes in the region, however, the competition authority is embedded in a ministry as a government department (or is under the strict supervision of the prime minister). In these cases, the competition authority remains budget-dependent or administratively dependent on government ministries under different forms of accountability.

The design of a competition agency has a decisive influence on the type and quality of policy outcomes that a country's competition regime achieves. An independent agency with a specific mandate and predictable decision making that remains consistent through a change of government will be better able to limit the extent that business groups can lobby ministries for favorable treatment, and will provide business with greater regulatory certainty.

Competition authorities operate within a wide variety of institutional frameworks. Under the *bifurcated judicial model*, the competition agency has investigative powers and must bring enforcement actions before the general courts. This is the model followed by the U.S. Antitrust Division of the Department of Justice (DoJ). In practice, the DoJ opens a formal enforcement proceeding, whether criminal or civil, carries out its investigation, and then brings the case before federal courts. While this model involves limited expertise in the adjudicative function, it offers the necessary detachment to ensure impartiality and transparency in the decision making. Problems associated with this model include the length and costs typically resulting from judicial litigation.

Under the bifurcated agency or tribunal model, the agency has investigative powers and brings enforcement actions before separate, specialized adjudicative authorities. This is the model followed by Canada with respect to noncriminal practices (for example, abuse of dominance, mergers, and

(continued on next page)

BOX 2.5

Institutional Design Models *Continued*

restrictive practices). The Canada Competition Bureau has investigative and enforcement functions while the Competition Tribunal, formed by federal judges and competition experts, performs adjudicative functions. The bifurcated agency and tribunal model provides a good level of independence as well as expertise in the adjudication. At the same time, it can tackle some of the procedural problems of general courts since the term to make a decision is normally shorter.

In the integrated agency model, a single specialized agency is entrusted with the investigative, enforcement, and adjudicative functions. Probably the best-known examples of such an agency are the U.S. Federal Trade Commission (FTC) and the Competition Directorate of the European Commission. The FTC investigates and adjudicates cases internally. Its decisions are then subject to court review—in the first instance before an administrative law judge whose decision can be appealed at the deferral court.

In the European Union, the Competition Directorate investigates and initially adjudicates competition cases subject to approval by the College of Commissioners. Parties have a right of appeal to the Court of First Instance and subsequently to the European Court of Justice. The advantages of this model are significant; it yields high levels of expertise both from the staff investigating the case and the body of commissioners adjudicating it. Additionally, this expertise not only assists in the adjudication of cases but also in the policy making of the agency. Integrated agencies offer also considerable advantages in terms of administrative efficiency. The main disadvantage of this model is related to the possible lack of impartiality in the adjudication of cases. Therefore, ensuring the necessary checks and balances to avoid any confusion between investigation and adjudication is crucial for integrated agencies.

Source: World Bank Competition Policy Team elaboration 2016.

Cooling-off periods for board members and key staff of competition authorities are not common across the region. A regime of incompatibilities and cooling-off periods should be part of the competition framework to safeguard independence of the competition authorities (figure 2.31). This is the prevailing solution in the selected European Union countries with board members performing their activities in exclusivity (except France where five out of seven board members can be market operators) and subject to an incompatibilities regime and a cooling-off period. MENA countries have no cooling-off periods (besides Egypt) and seldom require exclusivity (only Algeria and Kuwait) (figure 2.32).

FIGURE 2.31

Cooling-Off Periods for Board Members in MENA, 2015

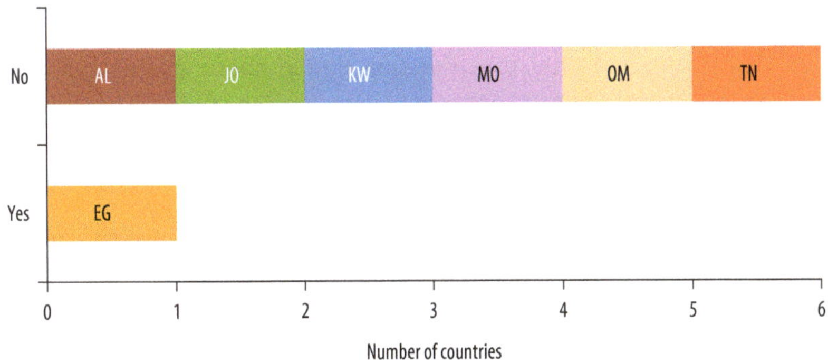

Source: World Bank Competition Policy Team 2015.
Note: AL = Algeria; EG = Egypt, Arab Rep.; JO = Jordan; KW = Kuwait; MENA = Middle East and North Africa; MO = Morocco; OM = Oman; TN = Tunisia.

FIGURE 2.32

Exclusivity for Board Members in MENA, 2015

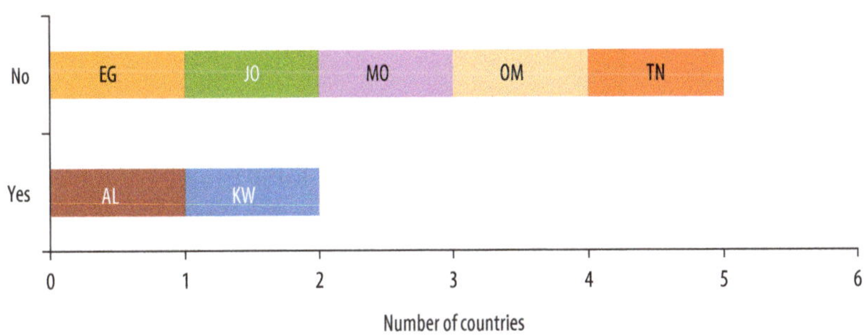

Source: World Bank Competition Policy Team 2015.
Note: AL = Algeria; EG = Egypt, Arab Rep.; JO = Jordan; KW = Kuwait; MENA = Middle East and North Africa; MO = Morocco; OM = Oman; TN = Tunisia.

Moreover, participation of government representatives (Morocco, Tunisia, Algeria, Jordan, and Egypt[25]) and private operators (Jordan, Morocco, Tunisia, and Egypt) in the competition agencies' boards are often accepted.[26]

From an operational perspective, sufficient financial resources, skilled staff, and effective powers of investigation and sanctioning can contribute to a better enforcement of competition law. To strengthen independence, good practice suggests that competition authorities' budgets be provided by parliament or that competition authorities move toward becoming at least partially self-financing in the longer term. The provision of a competition authority's budget by the minister of the ministry in which the agency is housed is generally considered to be suboptimal since it creates financial dependency that can damage the perceived independence and political neutrality of the agency. The amount of funds and how it is sourced determine how the competition authority is organized and whether it operates efficiently. Funding should not be an element that influences the decisions taken by the agency; instead, it should be sustainable and enable it to take decisions that are impartial and that it performs its mandate in an efficient and effective manner, namely in terms of staff hiring. The funding process should be simple, transparent, and efficient. In the MENA countries, there is a predefined budget normally allocated by the government (except Morocco and Egypt, where the budget is approved by the parliament). Most competition authorities have the power to recruit their own staff (except Oman; also Kuwait is still in the process of hiring staff). In the selected European Union countries, the budget figures are public and the agencies are provided with sufficient funding and staff to fulfill their mandate.[27] On the contrary, in the MENA countries, the competition authorities expressed concerns over insufficient resources—most of the MENA competition authorities have a staff of 20 or less, which may be insufficient to implement effectively their countries' competition policies.

Procedural Fairness and Transparency

Due process and transparency should be integral principles of the competition laws and are typically part of the mechanisms of accountability and transparency before Government and Parliament, the business community, and the public.

Separation between investigation and decision-making functions can provide additional warrantees against undue influence from both public and private entities. As such, this is the rule in the selected European Union countries and the exception in several MENA countries, in which such a functional separation between investigation and decision-making competences of the competition agencies is absent (except for Morocco, Egypt and Tunisia, in which this separation exists).

Moreover, transparency and accountability before the judiciary is essential to preserve the integrity of the competition agencies' decisions. In the MENA countries, the final decisions of the competition authorities are subject to judicial review (although this remains unclear in Oman). This is also the general rule in the European Union countries with a system characterized by independent judicial review, procedural transparency, and reporting before government and parliament. However, there is a lack of due process guarantees in the relationship to the competition

TABLE 2.14

Budget Allocation of Competition Authority in MENA, 2015

Parliament	Government	Government with parliament approval
Morocco	Algeria, Jordan, Kuwait, Tunisia	Egypt, Arab Rep.

Source: World Bank Competition Policy Team 2015.
Note: Information for Oman is not clearly reported.

TABLE 2.15

Accountability of Competition Authorities in MENA, 2015

Government minister	Parliament
Morocco, Algeria, Jordan, Kuwait, Oman, Tunisia	Egypt, Arab Rep.

Source: World Bank Competition Policy Team 2015.

authorities in some countries: (a) in Jordan, there are no provisions on oral hearings, access to nonconfidential version of statement of objections, and case files; (b) in Kuwait, fair and transparent procedures are to be defined in regulations developing the competition law; and (c) in Oman, the authority reportedly refuses access to a lawyer and commonly threatens lawful activities with incarceration.[28] With the exception of Egypt, competition authorities are only accountable to the government (see table 2.15).

Furthermore, safeguards that prevent the disclosure of confidential information to third parties are generally prevalent in the MENA countries similarly as with the European Union ones. Publicity of the agencies' decisions and activities should be ensured for transparency purposes before the public and businesses. This is the general rule in the European Union and MENA countries (with the exception of Oman for annual reports and reasoned decisions, and of Jordan for the latter). However, in some MENA countries the decisions are not always available online, which was the case for Algeria and Jordan. The decisions were available only until 2011 in Tunisia. For Egypt, the website was inoperative. Many MENA countries have not adopted guidelines (secondary legislation) explaining how they enforce provisions in their competition laws (Egypt, Jordan, and Morocco are exceptions), as shown in figure 2.33.

Moving Forward

Table 2.16 presents potential areas to make the competition legal framework less prone to undue influence and more effective in leveling

FIGURE 2.33

Availability of Guidelines for the Implementation of Competition Law to the Public in MENA, 2015

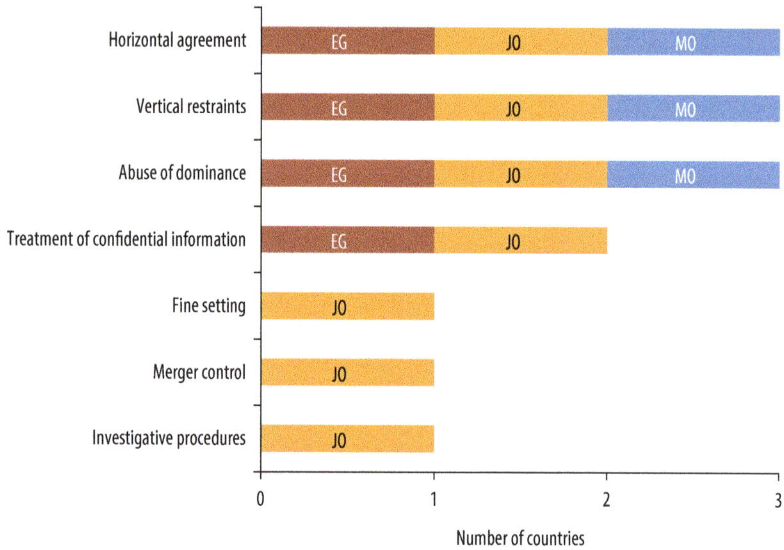

Source: World Bank Competition Policy Team 2015.
Note: EG = Egypt, Arab Rep.; JO = Jordan; MENA = Middle East and North Africa; MO = Morocco.

TABLE 2.16

Potential Areas for Making the Competition Legal Framework More Effective in MENA, 2015

	Algeria	Egypt, Arab Rep.	Jordan	Kuwait	Lebanon[a]	Morocco	Oman	Tunisia
The Competition Legal Framework								
Entry points for making the competition law more effective								
Adopt a comprehensive and effective competition law that applies to the main types of anticompetitive conduct and to all economic operators (public and private)					x			
Establish an efficient merger control regime in the competition law		x						
Expand the scope of the competition law to cover anticompetitive state action		x				x	x	
Eliminate/reduce competition law exceptions regarding:								
Conduct that is required/approved by other government authorities	x	x	x			x	x	x
Legal monopolies	x	x		x		x	x	x
Certain economic sectors, goods, or service	x	x		x		x	x	x
State bodies		x		x			x	
State-owned enterprises		x		x			x	
Professional associations						x		

(continued on next page)

TABLE 2.16

Potential Areas for Making the Competition Legal Framework More Effective in MENA, 2015 *Continued*

	Algeria	Egypt, Arab Rep.	Jordan	Kuwait	Lebanon[a]	Morocco	Oman	Tunisia
Eliminate the presumption of dominance (that is, criteria based on firms' market shares)			x	x			x	
Strengthen powers and tools to enforce competition law. In particular:								
Competition law provisions on leniency	x		x	x			x	
Establish adequate fines in the competition law (for example, up to 10 percent of firm's annual turnover in the affected market)	x		x					
Establish subpoena power							x	
Establish power to reach settlements	x		x	x			x	
Allow the competition agency to impose fines directly		x	x				x	
Establish a subsidy/state support control regime/ legislation to minimize competition distortions	x	x	x	x	x	x	x	x
Other potential entry points to enhance implementation								
Promote protocols of collaboration with sector regulators	x		x	x			x	x
Maintaining trust and independence in competition policy implementation								
Potential areas for making the competition law more effective								
Upgrade status of the competition agency from a government department to a body with administrative and financial autonomy			x					
Provide for an independent status of competition authority (for example, through the line ministry)	x	x	x	x		x	x	x
Eliminate/clarify the public interest test to approve mergers			x	x		x		x
Eliminate/reduce the possibility of having the line minister interfere with the decisions of the competition agency	x			x		x		x
Establish that board members should be appointed through an independent process	x	x	x	x		x	x	x
Establish clear rules regarding duration of board members' mandates			x				x	
Nominate board members at intervals	x	x		x		x	x	x
Establish objective criteria for appointment and dismissal of board members	x			x			x	
Impose rule of exclusivity of functions on board members and staff		x	x			x	x	x
Eliminate/minimize the presence of government representatives in the board	x	x	x			x		x
Consider reducing the presence of private sector representatives in the board		x	x			x		x
Put in place cooling-off periods after board members and staff leave the competition agency	x		x	x		x	x	x

(continued on next page)

TABLE 2.16

Potential Areas for Making the Competition Legal Framework More Effective in MENA, 2015 *Continued*

	Algeria	Egypt, Arab Rep.	Jordan	Kuwait	Lebanon[a]	Morocco	Oman	Tunisia
Other potential entry points to enhance implementation								
Ensure sustainable budget allocation (for example, from the parliament)	x		x	x			x	x
Ensure that the budget is sufficiently funded	x	x	x	x		x	x	x
Enable the competition authority to recruit its own staff							x	
Procedural Fairness and Transparency								
Potential areas for making the competition law more effective								
Make competition authorities accountable before the parliament and government (for example, present annual activity reports)	x		x	x		x	x	x
Separate investigative and decision-making functions	x		x	x			x	
Clarify in the competition law the right to judicial review							x	
Strengthen due process and rule of law in competition procedures (for example, in terms of oral hearings, access to nonconfidential version of statement of objections)			x	x			x	
Other potential entry points to enhance implementation								
Increase transparency mechanisms (for example, annual reports, publication of the decisions)	x		x				x	x
Ensure publicity of the competition authorities' activities and decisions, namely through online resources	x	x	x				x	x
Develop comprehensive competition bylaws for implementation/guidelines	x	x	x	x		x	x	x

Note: Blank cells signify that the box was not ticked.
a. In Lebanon, a competition law needs to be adopted and designed according to the guidelines provided throughout this section.

the playing field for both private and public players. This review provides only entry points into the analysis of those aspects that may give rise to undue private and public influence in the MENA countries. Hence, a more detailed analysis is required to provide a complete assessment of key competition policy issues, and contribute to increasing the effectiveness of the competition policy and legal framework implementation in tackling anticompetitive behavior and anticompetitive regulations and policies.

Conflict of Interest Restrictions

Conflict of interest refers to when an individual could exploit an official capacity for personal benefit, but has not done so yet. The presence of a conflict of interest is not an indicator of improper conduct, but rather a warning, or risk, of its possibility. Some of the most significant risks or conflicts of interest appear in the following situations:

- Stockholdings or private firm ownership
- Officials holding government contracts
- Gifts and hospitality
- Patronage or nepotism
- Private firm engagements (for example, board member, advisor, company officer)
- Outside employment with international organizations
- Voting on policy decisions
- Postemployment engagements

The operating principle of a conflict of interest system is to assist public officials in avoiding situations in which a conflict of interest could arise. Restrictions on conduct, incompatibilities, or engagements aim to prevent situations that frequently give rise to conflicts of interest. Restrictions place the burden of compliance on the public official, who must be aware of the laws, identify the situation, and act accordingly. Clear definitions of prohibited conduct reduce the pressure of uncertainty on public officials and employees by establishing a distinct line between acceptable and unacceptable activities. Policy makers and others must also provide a clear definition of conflict of interest and specify a broad prescription to avoid and resolve any perceived conflicts of interest that arise during performance of job tasks. In lieu of an enforceable code of conduct, this broad restriction on conflicts of interest encourages public officials to consider the effect that private interests may have on the public's perception of their ethics as representatives of the state. It also provides a means of reprimanding officials who violate the spirit of the law, rather than specific provisions or restrictions on behavior.

Countries worldwide have struggled over the past two decades to design and implement effective systems of conflict of interest. Cross-country analysis, such as the one produced by the World Bank,[29] highlights gaps that still exist in the existing systems and especially between the regulations and laws defining the system and their implementation. The World Bank Public Accountability Mechanisms (PAM) dataset found that nearly all countries specify conflict of interest restrictions for public officials, but the types of restriction, and which officials are subject to them, vary widely.

The MENA countries studied in this analysis (Jordan, Tunisia, Lebanon, Algeria, Morocco, Kuwait, Egypt, and Oman) scored as good or better on conflict of interest restrictions, as compared with the four European countries studied (France, Italy, Portugal, and Spain). In terms of average scores displayed in figure 2.34, MENA countries scored comparably to the four European countries, with the exception of monitoring and oversight. Overall country scores (figure 2.35) on conflict of interest restrictions do not cluster by region. Algeria has a very comprehensive conflict of interest regime based on restrictions, as do France and Portugal. But the average score for the remaining countries is 45 out of 100.

Figure 2.36 demonstrates that there is a wide variety of scores for subcategories, except for the coverage of public officials. Sanctions and oversight arrangements are often specified by law, but it is unclear whether sanctions are regularly applied, and what kind of monitoring and guidance that authorities provide to officials.

The underlying data highlight that civil servants are most often subject to conflict of interest restrictions, while heads of state are least likely to be required to modify behavior based on private interests. This finding corresponds to the World Bank Public Accountability Mechanisms (PAM) data, in which heads of state face fewer restrictions, and civil servants are subject to extensive restrictions. While it is often difficult to

FIGURE 2.34

Average Scores on Conflict of Interest Restrictions in MENA and European Comparators, 2015

0–100 scale, in which higher scores reflect more robust frameworks

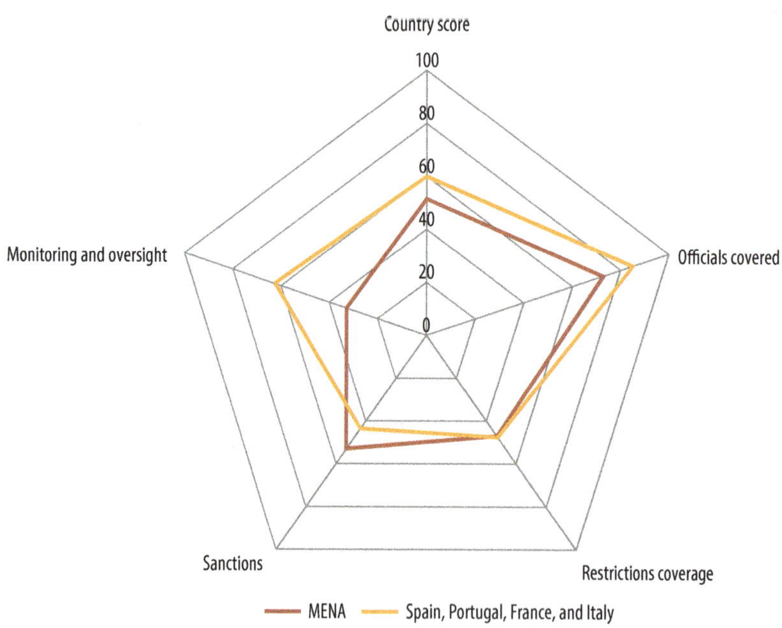

FIGURE 2.35

Overall Scores on Conflict of Interest Restrictions in MENA and European Comparators, 2015

0–100 scale, in which higher scores reflect more robust frameworks

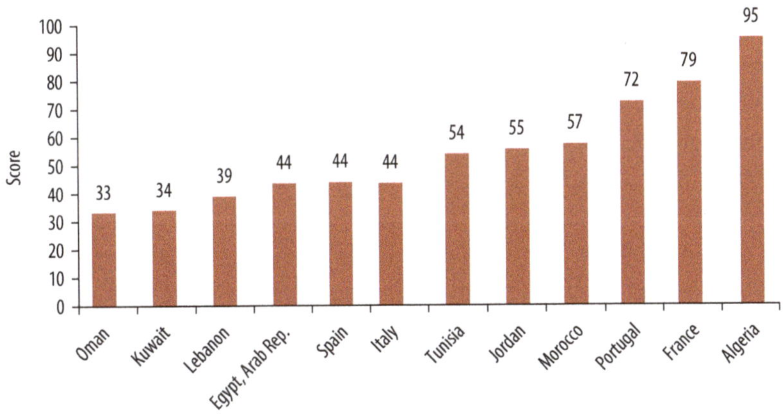

FIGURE 2.36

Scores on Conflict of Interest Restrictions in MENA and European Comparators, 2015

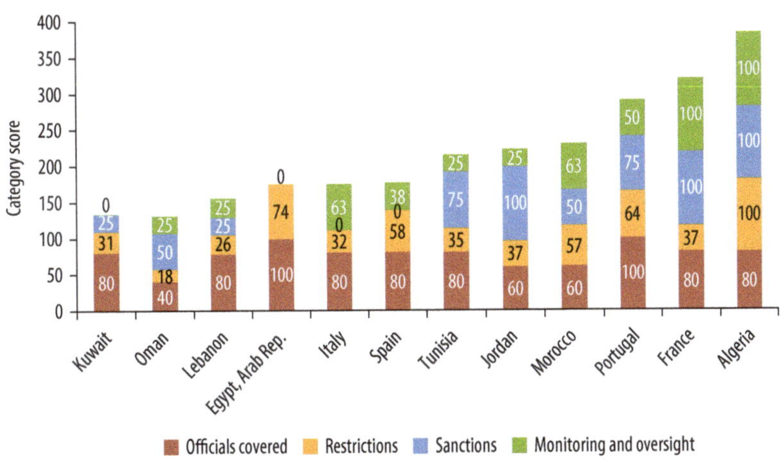

regulate the activities of members of parliament and ministers, as they cycle in and out of office with regularity, some activities that clearly represent risks to the appearance of high ethical standards should be restricted. Business activities are the most heavily restricted of private interests for ministers, members of parliament, and civil servants, with around 70 percent of both MENA and European countries regulating this type of conflict. This figure is similar to the World Bank PAM findings, with around 60 percent of countries regulating these restrictions. These types of business activities include holding government contracts, private firm ownership and stockholdings (except for members of parliament), and private firm board membership. The presence of these restrictions points to the recognition that private sector engagements may often conflict with public service mandates, particularly when public officials are responsible for selecting contractors and crafting policy. Membership in nongovernmental organizations (NGOs) and labor unions are the least likely activities to be restricted, indicating that participation in civil society is not considered a potential risk for misuse of office, even if it reflects an official's political leanings.

Postemployment restrictions are virtually nonexistent across the entire dataset, except for civil servants. This reflects the findings from the World Bank PAM dataset, in which only 30 percent of countries regulate employment after leaving office. Although it is possible for countries to require disclosure of employment opportunities after leaving office, a cooling-off period that prohibits employment with specific firms or fields may be more likely to discourage misuse of the authority and connections that are accorded to public officials while they are in office.

Addressing conflicts of interest through disclosure requirements is less common than restricting behavior (see figure 2.37, panels a–d). Disclosure systems require significant capacity for receipt and review of declaration forms, as well as the existence of trained personnel who can work with officials to alleviate conflicts. For countries unable to dedicate substantial financial and human resources to a disclosure system, postemployment restrictions are a cost-effective means of removing potential abuse of office. However, these restrictions must be coupled with appropriate sanctions and enforcement capabilities to be effective. Unfortunately, sanctions for violations of the restrictions of behavior are specified by law in only half of the countries in the dataset. Conflict of interest restrictions will be largely ineffective without a credible threat of enforcement. Enforcement bodies for these types of restrictions are even less likely to be specified by law, except for civil servants (whose employment is already highly regulated by a civil service body).

Financial Disclosure

Financial disclosure systems require that public officials disclose their income, assets, and financial interests. They are intended for a variety of purposes, most fundamentally to prevent and to detect the abuse of public office for private gain. They also help to build a climate of integrity by (a) providing guidance to officials about the principles and behaviors of

FIGURE 2.37

Disclosures and Restrictions in Public Accountability Mechanisms in 90-Country Dataset, 2013

Percent

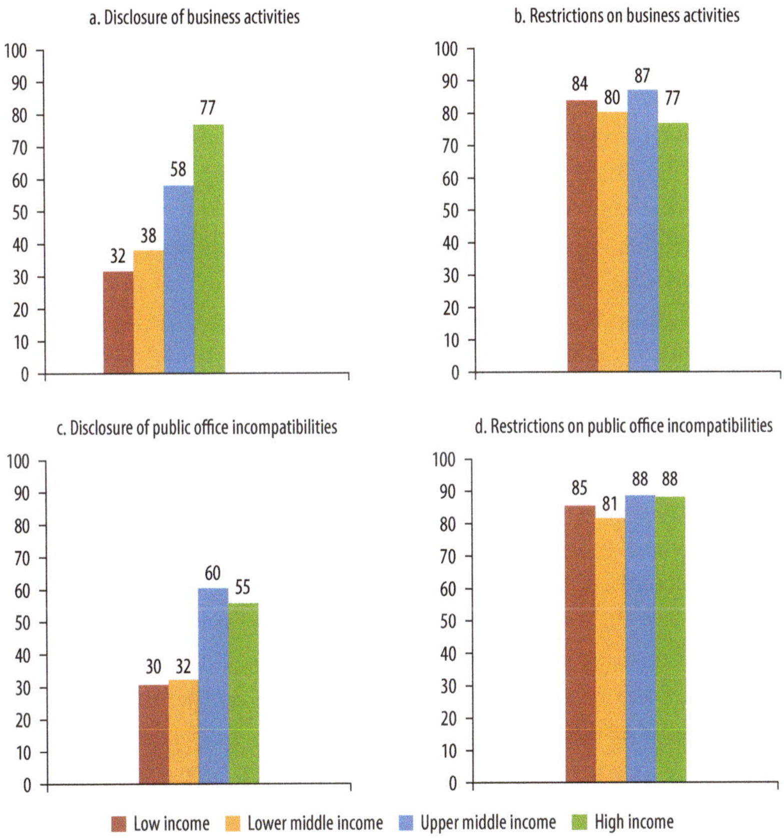

Source: World Bank PAM database 2013.

ethical conduct in public office, (b) reminding public officials that their behavior is subject to scrutiny, and (c) generating a valuable source of information for financial or corruption investigations. Most financial disclosure regimes combine prevention and detection, incorporating measures aimed at preventing conflicts of interests and abuse of office, as well as ways of detecting explicit disproportionate increases in wealth (also referred to as illicit enrichment).

Financial disclosure systems may focus on detecting instances of illicit enrichment by requiring public officials to disclose the ownership of real estate, moveable assets, cash, amounts and sources of income, and liabilities. This information can then be compared with land and vehicle registries, private firm registries, bank account information, tax databases, and the results of lifestyle checks by independent agencies or civil society. This approach can function as preventative, since the threat of detection serves as a deterrent to behavior that enriches officials at the expense of their public service.

Preventative measures are primarily focused on preventing and remedying conflicts of interest between an official's employment responsibilities and private financial interests. A preventative approach that focuses on conflicts of interest can be collaborative—encouraging participation of both employer and employee in a discussion about appropriate behavior and solutions to potential conflicts, without the immediate threat of sanction. The types of conflicts that might be disclosed include stockholdings; gifts and hospitality; private firm board membership; performing advisory services; serving as company officer of private firm, NGO, or labor union membership; holding outside employment or government contracts; and postemployment endeavors.

An effective disclosure system requires officials to disclose any interests that may compromise their ability to serve as unbiased agents of the public service. Disclosures can be divided into (a) ad hoc: disclosing private interest when a conflict arises with public interest; and (b) preventative: declaring one's private interest in advance of any conflict arising. Disclosures allow governments to monitor potential or existing conflicts, provide officials with regular reminders to review their circumstances for potential conflicts, and provide them with guidance on how to identify and avoid them. A disclosure system involves the participation of both public officials and their supervisors (or other ethics authority figures) in the identification of potential or actual conflicts, so that these conflicts may be resolved efficiently and effectively.

Many countries have preventative systems that have evolved from restriction-based models to a hybrid model that incorporates some form of disclosure. In disclosure systems, conflicts can be addressed in a number of ways, depending on the nature of the conflict and the responsibilities of the official:

- Divestiture of the investments and interests
- Cessation of further acquisition of the investments or interests
- Freezing any investment transaction for a specified period of time
- Placement of the investment in a blind trust (without the requirement to first divest from current investments)
- Cessation from handling cases with actual or potential conflict of interest
- Reassignment of duties (to another individual) that pose actual or potential conflict of interest
- Prohibition of information flow regarding actual or potential conflict of interest

The World Bank PAM dataset finds that nearly 80 percent of countries have some sort of financial disclosure framework, but their features vary significantly across income. Higher income countries tend to have more sophisticated verification systems, whereas lower income countries face resource constraints in monitoring and oversight arrangements. Upper-middle-income countries specify considerable items to be disclosed in terms of assets, liabilities, and interests. It is interesting to note that ministers, members of parliament, and civil servants are subject to financial disclosure obligations more often in middle-income countries (MICs).

MENA countries scored comparably to the European countries included in the study, with the exception of public access to declarations, as illustrated in figure 2.38. Overall country scores on financial disclosure do not cluster by region. France has a very comprehensive financial disclosure regime, whereas the Algeria, Lebanon, and Portugal scores fall into the middle performers range. The average score for the remaining countries is 50 out of 100 (figure 2.39).

Heads of state are least likely to be subject to financial disclosure provisions, since monarchies are exempt from legal provisions of this nature. However, there is high prevalence of financial disclosure regimes for

FIGURE 2.38

Average Scores on Financial Disclosure Restrictions for MENA and European Comparators, 2015

0–100 scale, in which higher scores reflect more robust frameworks

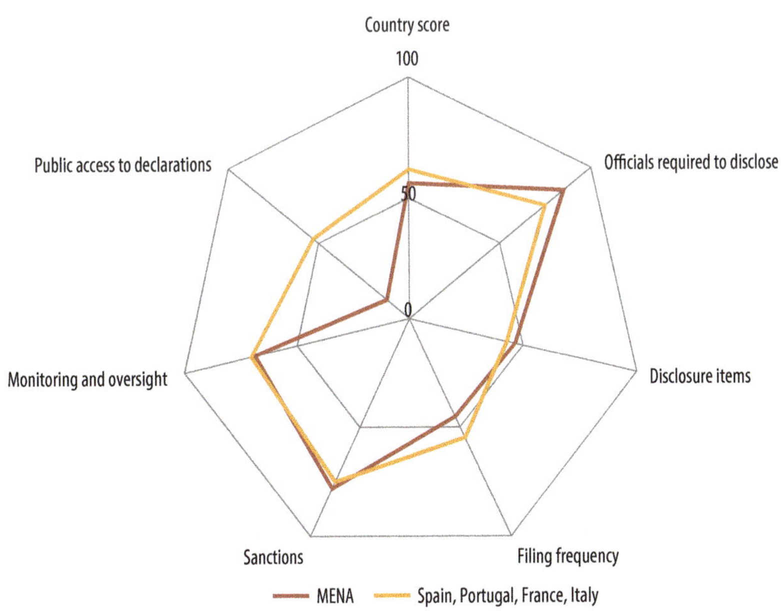

FIGURE 2.39

Overall Financial Disclosure Scores for MENA and European Comparators, 2015

0–100 scale, in which higher scores reflect more robust frameworks

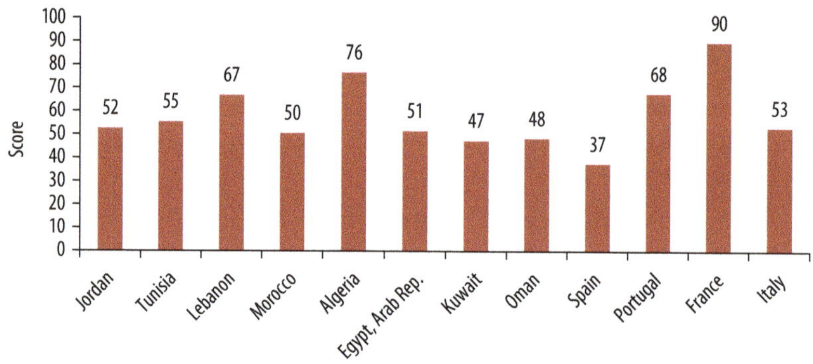

members of parliament, ministers, and civil servants in MENA countries. These public officials are required to disclose the following:

- Real estate
- Movable assets
- Cash
- Loans and debts
- Income from outside employment and assets
- Gifts
- Private firm ownership or stock holdings

In contrast to MENA countries, the European countries do not have a high instance of requiring cash, loans, and debts to be disclosed, and they are less likely to require civil servants to disclose income, assets, and interests than members of parliament and ministers. This may be because civil servants are subject to extensive conflict of interest restrictions rather than financial disclosure regimes.

Public officials are required to file declarations upon taking and leaving office in most MENA countries. However, ad hoc and annual filings are not common. This is unfortunate, since annual filing allows for periodic review of changes in assets, income, and interests. In the absence of this kind of extensive process to verify the veracity of declarations, ad hoc disclosure of conflicts allows managers and ethics advisors to immediately address issues. This is particularly important in voting and decision making, for example, for members of parliament and civil servants overseeing contracts and public policy.

Sanctions, monitoring, and oversight are specified by law in nearly all countries in the dataset (figure 2.40). This is encouraging, since financial disclosure regimes focused on detecting instances of illicit enrichment require a credible threat of detection and credible threat of sanctions to be effective. However, it is not clear if all financial disclosure regimes are functioning in practice. In cases in which an enforcement body is specified, the World Bank PAM dataset has shown that a specialized commission is the most common. These commissions tend to have independent budgets, and in some cases independent policing powers and investigative capacities, which can help ensure greater effectiveness of the financial disclosure system. In any case, an oversight agency or department should be established for enforcement of rules, issuance of guidance materials, and monitoring of implementation. Ethics advisors, either within agencies or in specialized commissions, should be appointed to provide guidance to officials on specific instances of conflict avoidance.

Although the opportunities for abuse of public office might increase as economies develop in complexity, the risk for misuse of authority exists at all levels of income and responsibility. With a credible threat of enforcement, restrictions may serve as a practical first step to addressing the potential for misconduct. As capacity grows, the addition of disclosure requirements can help to instill and reinforce a sense of ethics in the public service. This is particularly true when disclosure regimes are collaborative, with the aim of identifying and mitigating conflicts of interest, rather than punishing public officials for impropriety.

FIGURE 2.40

Category Scores on Financial Disclosure for MENA and European Comparators, 2015

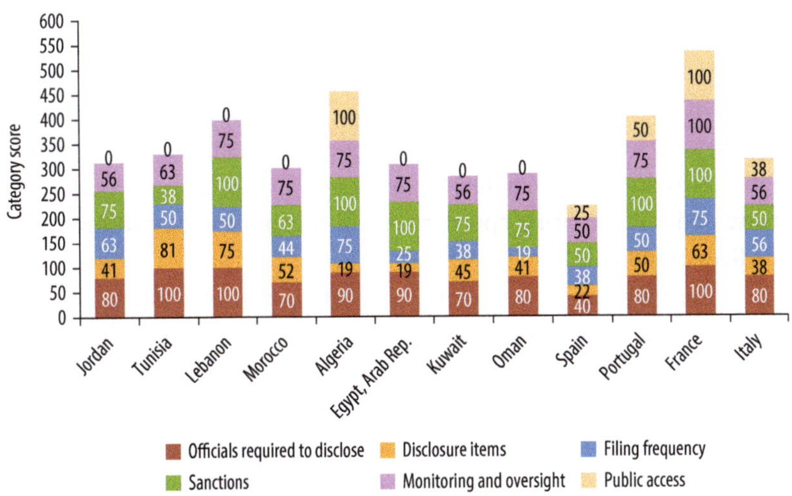

Unfortunately, MENA countries fall quite short with regard to public access to declarations (figure 2.40). Only Algeria allows access to declaration content, consisting of only assets, through publication in the official journal, *National Gazette*. European countries provide for requests for declaration content, and in many cases, publish content on a dedicated website that allows download for analysis and reuse. While public availability of declaration content will never replace the need for government capacity and expertise in overseeing the financial disclosure system, it reinforces the pressure for public officials to exhibit ethical behavior with regard to the intersection of their private interests and the public interest.

Freedom of Information

Freedom of information systems function as an integral, foundational factor in the institutionalization of transparency. Freedom of information, as a right and a principle, entrenches the notion of transparency as part of good government. Freedom of information systems (also known as right to information and access to information) are practical components of government administration that reflect commitment to the principle of transparency, and may serve to encourage, if not facilitate, participation and accountability.

Although freedom of information systems are only a part of transparency in government, they are a substantial factor in successful institutionalization of openness and access to information. A freedom of information system aims to increase the transparency of government by providing regular and reliable information to the public and facilitating appropriate and relevant use of that information. Experts commonly support the notion that access to information is integral to the promotion of participation, transparency, and accountability in any given society. A freedom of information framework aims at improving the efficiency of the government and increasing the transparency of its functioning by the following: (a) regularly and reliably providing government documents to the public; (b) educating the public on the significance of transparent government; and (c) facilitating appropriate and relevant use of information in the lives of individuals.

Furthermore, to act as an effective anticorruption tool, freedom of information depends upon a legally entrenched right to access documents held by the government (and in some cases, by private bodies). Access to information can be protected through a variety of legal mechanisms, from explicit constitutional safeguards to individual departmental orders. For a framework to be an effective and functioning mechanism for transparency, seven factors are key: (a) scope of coverage of disclosures; (b) procedures for accessing information; (c) exemptions to disclosure requirements; (d) enforcement mechanisms; (e) specified deadlines for release of requested information; (f) sanctions for noncompliance; and (g) proactive disclosure.

The World Bank PAM dataset finds that existence of freedom of information laws is closely tied to the level of income. Only 30 percent of lower income countries have freedom of information regimes in place, contrasted with nearly 70 percent of upper-middle-income countries and 95 percent of high-income countries. In addition, the existence of an independent nonjudicial appeals mechanism, in the form of an information commissioner, is found in only 50 percent of countries. Most often, countries rely on first appeals at the level of the public body and second appeals in the regular courts, despite the implicit bias in the former process, and the high costs and level of expertise required at the second level.

Of the three corrective mechanisms in this study, access to information is the least developed and least entrenched in the MENA region (figure 2.41). Compared to the European countries included in the study, MENA countries score poorly. Overall country scores on access to information cluster somewhat by region. European countries and Tunisia

FIGURE 2.41

Average Scores on Access to Information in MENA and European Comparators, 2015

0–100 scale, in which higher scores reflect more robust frameworks

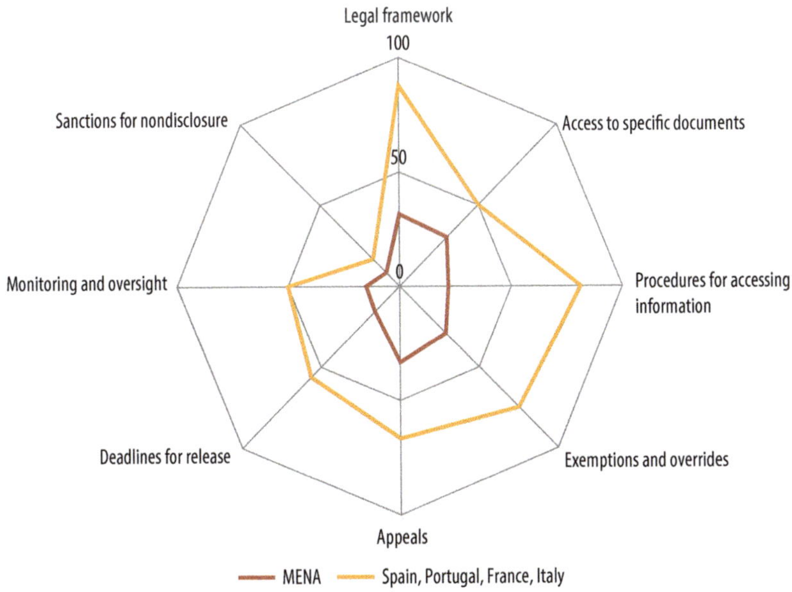

score greater than 50 points, whereas Jordan, Lebanon, and Morocco score less than 50. The remaining four MENA countries of Algeria, Egypt, Kuwait, and Oman score at or near zero; none of these countries have an access to information law that establishes a legal right to information and the framework for releasing information (figure 2.42). Of the documents analyzed in this study, enacted legal instruments are the most likely to be legally required for disclosure in MENA countries, with draft laws and annual budgets a close second. In European countries, these documents are often released online proactively, regardless of whether it is prescribed by law. However, this leaves citizens with little basis to demand information should it not be released for any reason.

In countries with a dedicated access to information law, guidelines for release of information are common, which allow for both written and electronic submission of requests. However, despite the international standard of a 20-day response deadline, none of the MENA countries specified any deadlines for responding to information requests. This is unfortunate, given that requiring the release of information within specified deadlines lays the groundwork for applying sanctions in cases of noncompliance. Often this is the consequence of vague or sparse legislation that does not provide substantive instructions for the implementation and enforcement of the right to information.

All countries with a dedicated law have specific exemptions to disclosure, including European countries. However, balancing tests that provide mechanisms to override these exemptions are not common in MENA countries; only Lebanon and Tunisia provide for this practice by law.

FIGURE 2.42

Overall Country Scores on Access to Information in MENA and European Comparators, 2015

0–100 scale, in which higher scores reflect more robust frameworks

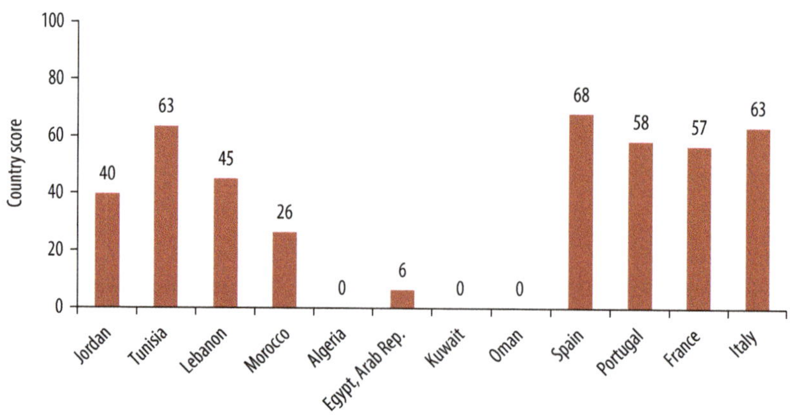

When the public interest in maintaining the exemption outweighs the public interest in the disclosure of the information, then the information can be withheld. If the public interest in disclosing the information is equal to or greater than the public interest in maintaining the exemption, then the information must be disclosed. A related harm test may allow only relevant bodies to withhold specific information in cases in which there is legitimate risk that release of the information would cause harm. The World Bank PAM Initiative finds that balancing tests are more prevalent with increasing country income levels, most likely because these tests require trained professionals to apply the law in complex cases (figure 2.43).

In contrast with all of the European countries in this study, only Jordan and Tunisia require that information officers be appointed in public agencies. They are also the only MENA countries with laws that identify a nodal agency to oversee implementation of access to information in the public sector. Nodal agencies or departments are responsible for oversight of the access to information regime, including training of

FIGURE 2.43

Category Scores on Access to Information in MENA and European Comparators, 2015

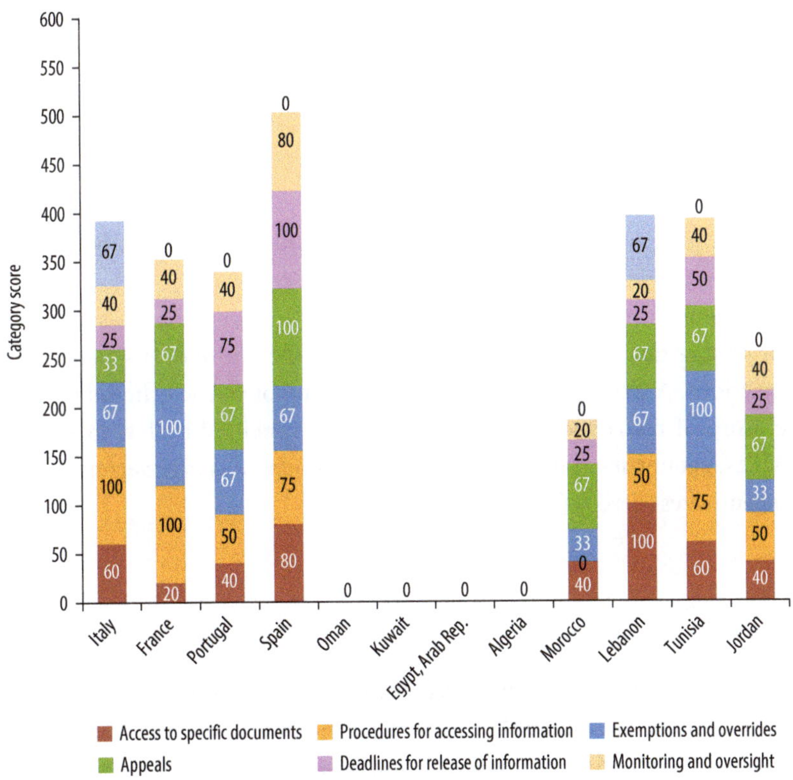

FIGURE 2.44

Appeal Mechanisms in Access to Information Frameworks in 90-Country Dataset, 2010

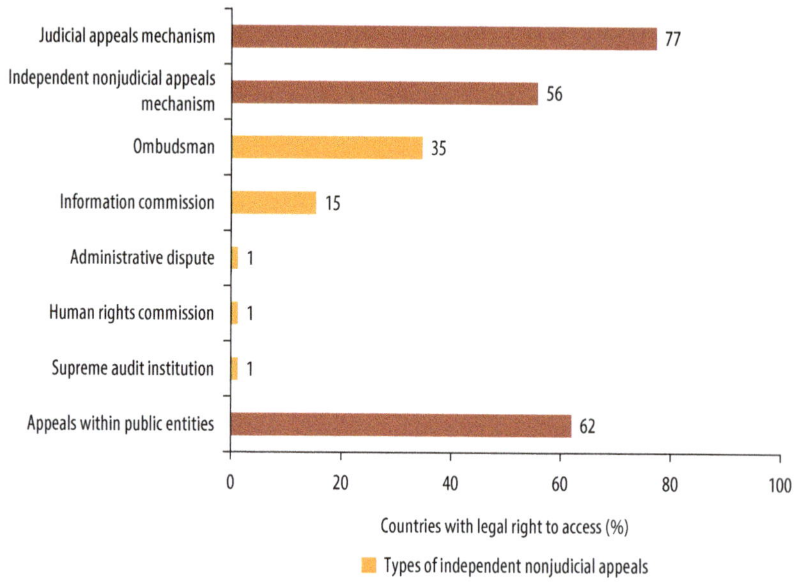

Source: World Bank PAM database 2013.

civil servants and information awareness campaigns for the public. None of the MENA countries specified an independent enforcement agency to handle appeals. Worldwide, the most common means of nonjudicial enforcement is the Information Commission through the hearing of appeals. Unlike ombudsmen, commissions of this type often have the authority to force disclosure of government agencies, even if they do not have sanctioning powers. Nearly all countries allow for appeals to be heard by the courts, but this should be a last resort, given the high costs and lengthy processing times for judicial cases.

Sanctions in access to information regimes are not common, so it is not surprising that only two of the countries in the entire data set specified sanctions. A worrying trend is the sanctioning of public officials for disclosure of restricted information, which is specified by law in several MENA countries. This practice discourages openness in government and incentivizes secrecy (figure 2.44).

Summary

The data for this study suggest that in all MENA countries, the policy environment is vulnerable to privilege seeking. However, the degree varies by countries and within countries, by policy areas. Table 2.17

TABLE 2.17

Privilege Resistance Summary Scores in Policy Making in MENA, 2015

Average

	Policy areas	Public accountability	All areas
Country	1	2	3
Algeria	0.628	0.669	0.642
Egypt, Arab Rep.	0.683	0.644	0.670
Jordan	0.593	0.429	0.538
Kuwait	0.482	0.270	0.411
Lebanon	0.539	0.444	0.507
Morocco	0.715	0.462	0.630
Oman	0.556	0.371	0.494
Tunisia	0.610	0.504	0.574

Note: The maximum possible score is 1.

FIGURE 2.45

Privilege Resistance of Policy Making in MENA, 2015

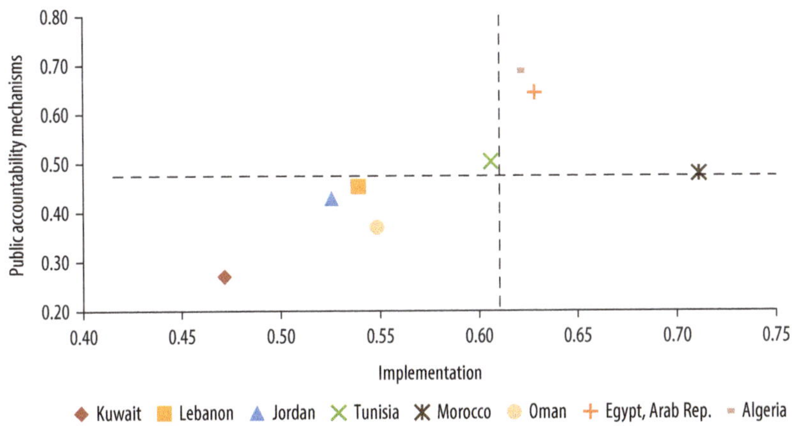

presents the average scores for six policy areas (trade and customs, business regulations, allocation of public land, public procurement, investment incentives, and access to finance) and the three dimensions of public accountability (conflict of interest regulations, asset disclosure, and freedom of information) covered by this study. Table 2.17 also presents the average scores covering all these nine areas.

Given the limitations of the methodology and data (as described in chapter 1), finer differences in table 2.17 should be ignored; rather the focus should be on the big picture that these data reveal (see figure 2.45). First, the average scores for the six policy areas (shown in column 1) confirm that in all MENA countries the policy environment is vulnerable to privilege seeking. It is possible to group the eight countries into two categories: (a) moderately vulnerable to privilege seeking: Algeria, Egypt, Morocco, and Tunisia, although Morocco and Tunisia have weaker accountability mechanisms and are less protected against privilege-seeking behavior; and (b) substantially vulnerable: Jordan, Kuwait, Lebanon, and Oman.

A high degree of accountability for public officials may dilute the incentive of officials to grant privilege in exchange for favors by increasing the costs of doing so. Thus, to some extent, it may mitigate the vulnerabilities in the policy areas. However, the likelihood of that happening in the MENA region is rather poor because of the low degree of accountability. This is indicated by the average scores for the three dimensions of public accountability covered by this study. As shown in column 2 of table 2.17, no MENA country scores above 0.70. Indeed, with the exception of Algeria and Egypt, all countries score 0.50 or below, with Oman and Kuwait scoring particularly low. This suggests that the vulnerability to privilege—as indicated by the assessment of individual policy areas—may be accentuated because of poor checks and balances on public officials. In this regard, Morocco's top score on the policy areas (0.715) does not give much comfort given its poor score on public accountability (0.462).

Last, it may be noted that there are variations in privilege vulnerability across policy areas, both overall and in individual countries. The best score is for trade and customs in Morocco (0.908) and the worst is for allocation of public land in Kuwait (0.20). Overall, the vulnerability to privilege seeking is the worst in public land allocation with an average score of 0.393 across the countries. Relatively better areas are trade and customs (0.726) and access to finance (0.712); nonetheless, this is not comforting given the absolute levels of the scores. These wide variations suggest considerable scope for improvement as well as the scope for learning from relative good practices in and across countries.

Notes

1. This is particularly true of nontariff barriers, which are often introduced in a discretionary manner to provide protection to favored groups or even individual businesses.
2. The *Systematic Country Diagnostic for Tunisia* (World Bank 2015c) states: "Tunisia has relatively low nontariff measures (NTMs) frequency and coverage ratios, but it has highly bureaucratic and potentially discretionary procedures. Firms have repeatedly complained about the lack of transparency in the application of rules giving room to procedural inefficiencies, obstructions, and arbitrary conduct hampering the country's overall competitiveness."

3. According to World Bank (2015b): "Discretionary implementation of customs regulations and tariff evasion results in an estimated annual revenue loss of at least US$100 million (approximately 0.15 percent of GDP). Moreover, import-monopolists (i.e., firms that are the only firms that import particular products) on average underreport in the magnitude of 131 percent relative to firms that are not. Corruption in customs has received considerable media attention and has also been identified as one of the key mechanisms by which cronies were able to reap rents."
4. Future work may look at other regulatory areas. These may include very specific regulatory interfaces, such as the transparency and fairness in the provision of vendor permits or specific regulatory transactions and inspection practices in the hospitality industry. Such areas are economically important, and are important for developing trust between regulators (the state) and economic agents (citizens).
5. The "intrinsic" scope for discretionary behavior depends on the nature of the regulatory interface and is independent of the policy and administrative regime in a country. Given the inherent scope, the actual scope for discretionary behavior is a function of the policy and administrative regime of the country.
6. Oman data are incomplete and do not allow us to draw conclusions.
7. For more details on competition advocacy, see ICN (2009).
8. Consistent with the World Bank Markets and Competition Policy Assessment Tool (MCPAT), government interventions are described so as to include government policies, regulations, rules, procedures, and actions of government officials that affect decisions made by market players regarding economic matters.
9. Procompetitive regulations are those that are designed to achieve public policy objectives while minimizing the extent to which the regulation hinders competition, or those that are set with the explicit objective of increasing entry or the degree of rivalry in a market.
10. This framework includes the following principles: (a) role clarity, (b) preventing undue influence and maintaining trust, (c) decision making and governing body structure for independent regulators, (d) accountability and transparency, (e) engagement, (f) funding and (g) performance evaluation. (OECD 2014).

    See also the following documents of relevance: OECD *Revolving Doors, Accountability and Transparency—Emerging Regulatory Concerns and Policy Solutions in the Financial Crisis* (May 5, 2009); OECD *Institutional Design of Competition Authorities—Note by Allan Fells and Henry Ergas* (December 18, 2014); OECD *Summary Record of the Roundtable on Changes in Institutional Design* (March 23, 2015); OECD *Draft Report of Best Practice Principles for Improving Regulatory Enforcement and Inspections* (2013).
11. Article 42 of the Treaty on the Functioning of the European Union establishing that the legislator can modify the standard competition rules when applying them to the agriculture value chain (in addition, the French law explicitly excludes agriculture from the remit of the competition law). The competition rules for agricultural products (other than fisheries products) are set out in Regulation 1308/2013 (the "Common Market Organisation (CMO) Regulation"). Pursuant to the regulation, it establishes that competition rules apply to agricultural products except in limited cases:

(a) when anticompetitive agreements are necessary to achieve the objectives of the Common Agriculture Policy (CAP) or (b) when they are implemented by farmers' associations or producer organizations and concern the production and sale of agricultural products or the use of joint facilities for the storage, treatment or processing of agricultural products—in any case, this second exemption does not apply to agreements, decisions and practices which entail an obligation to charge an identical price or to exclude competition.

12. Despite the absence of merger control powers, the Egyptian Competition Authority has held discussions with the Health Ministry surrounding mergers in the sector that could lead to the creation of dominant positions in the health care market. In addition, Kuwait's competition law does not specifically include vertical agreements but this does not necessarily mean that the competition law will not be enforced in relation to this type of agreements.
13. It is worth highlighting the advocacy efforts carried out by the Egyptian Competition Authority, which signed cooperation agreements with the Egyptian Legislative Reform Committee and the Egyptian Regulatory Reform and Development Activity on the review and streamlining of business-related regulations.
14. Construction materials, telecommunications, financial services, transportation, insurance, auditing, and foodstuffs.
15. Cooking oils, cement, and professional services.
16. Six market studies including in the following sectors: media, food industries, telecommunications, and books for schools.
17. *Leniency* refers to the partial or total exoneration from the penalties that would otherwise be applicable to a cartel member that reports its cartel membership to a competition enforcement agency.
18. In Jordan, Algeria, and Oman, the court may consider when deciding the penalty if the violator provided information leading to the uncovering of the practice.
19. The board of the Competition Authority can enforce only cease and desist orders; for competition law violations, it must bring enforcement actions against violators before the Economic Courts (although the Competition Authority's chairperson has the power to settle violations).
20. Published in World Bank (forthcoming).
21. Typically, provisions on price controls in the competition laws are referring to exceptional situations, which are limited in time (this is also the case in France). However, the practice in some MENA countries shows that such provisions may provide an opportunity for the introduction of unlimited price controls through other laws (for example, in Tunisia).
22. France is an exception in this regard with the law establishing that prices may be regulated by decree of the Council of State (Conseil d'Etat) after consulting the authority in industries or areas in which price competition is limited either by monopoly situations, by lasting supply difficulties, or by legislative or regulatory provisions.
23. Not applicable in the case of Spain where the competition authority and sector regulators are integrated within a single authority: Comisión Nacional de Mercados y Competencia (CNMC).
24. On the other hand, the Egyptian Competition Authority recently entered into protocols with the Telecoms Regulator and the Financial Surveillance

Authority, in addition to ensuring presence in the board of the Electricity Regulator.

25. The 2014 review of the competition law in Egypt reduced the number of government representatives in the board from four to two.
26. Note: information for Oman is not clearly reported.
27. In the European Union, agencies have financial autonomy and may allocate freely their budget and recruit their own staff. However, there is no homogeneity in terms of sources of funding and budget approval regime: in Portugal and Italy, the authorities are self-financed: in the first case, through a transfer of revenues from other regulatory authorities (budget subject to ministerial preapproval) and in the second case, through a mandatory contribution from companies incorporated in Italy whose turnover exceeds a threshold of €50 million. On the other hand, in France and Spain, the budget is allocated by the parliament and is based upon state funding.
28. See the Sultanate of Oman website, http://www.state.gov/documents/organization/236828.pdf.
29. World Bank PAM Initiative. More information, see PAM's website, http://www.agidata.org/pam.

References

Ayadi, Lotfi, Nancy Benjamin, Sami Bensassi, and Gaël Raballand. 2013. "Estimating Informal Trade across Tunisia's Land Borders." World Bank Policy Research Working Paper 6731, World Bank, Washington, DC.

Farazi, Subika, Erik Feyen, and Roberto Rocha. 2011. "Bank Ownership and Performance in the Middle East and North Africa Region." World Bank WPS5620. Washington, DC: World Bank.

ICN (International Competition Network). 2009. "Report on Assessment of ICN Members' Requirements and Recommendations on Further ICN Work on Competition Advocacy." Presented at the 8th Annual Conference of the ICN, Zurich, June.

Ivaldi, Marc, Frédéric Jenny, and Aleksandra Khimich. 2016. "Cartel Damages to the Economy: An Assessment for Developing Countries." In *Competition Law Enforcement in the BRICS and in Developing Countries*, edited by Frederic Jenny and Yannis Katsoulacos, 103–33. New York: Springer.

Kirkpatrick, Grant. 2009. "The Corporate Governance Lessons from the Financial Crisis." *OECD Journal: Financial Market Trends* 1.

Kitzmuller, Markus, and Martha Martinez Licetti. 2012. "Competition Policy: Encouraging Thriving Markets for Development." Viewpoint Note Number 331. World Bank, Washington, DC.

Litan, Robert E., Michael Pomerleano, and Vasudevan Sundararajan, eds. 2002. *Financial Sector Governance: The Role of the Public and Private Sectors*. Washington, DC: Brookings Institution Press.

Motta, Massimo. 2004. *Competition Policy*. Cambridge, U.K.: Cambridge University Press.

OECD (Organsiation for Economic Co-operation and Development). 2010. *Methodology for Assessing Procurement Systems*. Paris: OECD.

———. 2014. *Best Practice Principles on the Governance of Regulators.* Paris: OECD. http://www.oecd.org/gov/regulatory-policy/governance-regulators.htm

Ottow, Annetje. 2015. *Market and Competition Authorities: Good Agency Principles.* Oxford, U.K.: Oxford University Press.

Rijkers, Bob, Caroline Freund, and Antonio Nucifora. 2014. "All in the Family: State Capture in Tunisia." Policy Research Working Paper 6810. World Bank, Washington, DC.

Shen, Xiaofang, and Xiaolun Sun. 2012. *Untying the Land Knot.* Washington, DC: World Bank.

World Bank. 2009. *From Privilege to Competition: Unlocking Private-Led Growth in the Middle East and North Africa.* Washington, DC: World Bank.

———. 2011. *Financial Access and Stability: A Road Map for the Middle East and North Africa.* Washington, DC: World Bank.

———. 2013. *Global Financial Development Report 2013: Rethinking the Role of the State.* Washington, DC: World Bank.

———. 2014a. *Jobs for Shared Prosperity: Time for Action in the Middle East and North Africa.* Washington, DC: World Bank.

———. 2014b. *Jobs or Privilege? Releasing Prosperity in the Middle East and North Africa.* Washington, DC: World Bank.

———. 2014c. *More Jobs, Better Jobs: A Priority for Egypt.* Washington, DC: World Bank.

———. 2014d. *Why Doesn't MENA Export More? A Firm-Level Perspective.* Washington, DC: World Bank.

———. 2015a. *Enabling Implementation of Public Procurement Reform in MENA Countries: A Case Study of Jordan and Morocco.* Washington, DC: World Bank.

———. 2015b. "Towards Capture-Resistant Private Sector Policymaking in MENA: Shielding Private Sector Policies from Privileges and Discretion: Policy Instruments and Operational Implications." T&C Concept Note, World Bank, Washington, DC.

———. 2015c. *Tunisia: Systematic Country Diagnostic.* Washington, DC: World Bank.

———. 2015d. *World Development Report 2015: Mind, Society and Behavior.* World Bank.

———. 2016b. "Benchmarking Public Procurement 2016 Report." World Bank, Washington, DC.

———. 2016c. "Markets and Competition Policy Assessment Toolkit." World Bank, Washington, DC.

———. 2017. "Benchmarking Public Procurement 2017 Report." World Bank, Washington, DC.

World Bank and ACF (Africa Competition Forum). 2016. *Breaking Down Barriers: Unlocking Africa's Potential through Vigorous Competition Policy.* Washington, DC: World Bank.

World Bank and OECD. 2017. *A Step Ahead: Competition for Shared Prosperity and Poverty Alleviation.* World Bank, Washington, DC.

CHAPTER 3

From Measurement to Action

Going Forward: An Operational Agenda

The analysis in chapter 2 reveals weaknesses in policy areas related to the private sector in the Middle East and North Africa (MENA) region that create opportunities for privilege seeking. As described in chapter 1, the database underpinning this analysis largely consists of indicator values for dimensions of the policy areas studied for eight MENA countries and four European comparator countries. These values are essentially binary numbers, which indicate whether certain features (for example, institutions, policies, or practices) exist for these policy dimensions. The values are based on the judgments of experts familiar with the respective policy areas in the countries. The experts were also provided with detailed guidance on how to perform their assessments. Nonetheless, binary scoring has its limitations. Some degree of subjectivity creeps into the assessments, and often there are gray areas that cannot be adequately captured by such scoring.

Thus, the findings of our analysis should be viewed as a first attempt to tackle this agenda from an operational point of view. Rather, the usefulness of the exercise lies in providing initial indications of where weaknesses may exist in the policy systems of these countries that create scope for privilege seeking. Such indications can convey where it may be worthwhile to probe further so that specific operational interventions could be identified to make the policy apparatus in a country resistant to privilege seeking.

Notwithstanding the methodological limitations, the approach of this study, including its wide coverage of countries and policy dimensions, provides important insights. For example, it brings out the role of synergy between policy dimensions. Thus, countries may have processes for rule-based decisions that help restrain privilege seeking. Despite this, the culture of rule-based decision making may be fragile because supporting features, such as grievance redress mechanisms and systems to fight fraudulent behavior, are weak or nonexistent. Even where such supporting mechanisms exist, they may be fragile in the absence of more fundamental governance features such as regular stakeholder consultation and public sharing of information. The analysis thus demonstrates both the synergy between different policy dimensions and a hierarchy among them.

The synergy between different policy dimensions may also create the possibility of a virtuous cycle of change. This suggests that a small set of politically feasible, technical solutions may trigger additional changes. This may generate the cumulative effect needed to make a significant dent in a privilege-ridden policy system. Such ripple effects are often driven by dynamics in governments. Thus, a reform action in one area can demonstrate the benefits of reform to stakeholders in the government, both functionaries in the agency performing the reform and in other parts of government. It may also show to risk-averse bureaucrats that actual risks of carrying out a reform are less than perceived, thus reducing their resistance to change. Thus, although the initial reform may be catalyzed by an external agent, such as a development partner, subsequent changes may be driven by internal dynamics in governments; however, external actors may continue to support the process, even if it is only through some timely nudges. Appendix C discusses these dynamics in detail with a summary subsequently provided.

The ripple effect of an initial reform may happen both vertically and horizontally. Consider the case of rule-based decision making in the allocation of public land and assume that a reform champion has introduced this discipline in the government. Once the benefit of this reform is demonstrated, the same reform champion or others involved in the allocation of public land may decide to consolidate the gains through additional reform, such as a grievance mechanism so that applicants for public land may voice their concerns or an appropriate policy and legal framework that will buttress the rule-based decision-making process.[1] At a later stage, the reformers who work on land allocation may become bolder and ready to become even more participatory and transparent. They may put in place, for example, mechanisms for stakeholder consultation and public sharing of information on allocation of public land. These are examples of a vertical spillover effect, that is, synergy within the same policy area.

The ripple effect may also happen horizontally, that is, by triggering reform dynamics in a different policy area. Thus, establishing a system of rule-based decision making in the allocation of public land may lead to establishing similar systems in other policy areas such as public procurement and business regulations. This second round of reform may be followed by a third round in which similar systems are introduced, such as for customs and trade and for investment incentives.

Sometimes, the rounds of ripple effects come full circle to the original reform. Thus, transparency measures in the area of land allocation may create pressure to sustain and strengthen the initial reform in land allocation, that is, the introduction of rule-based decision making. When that happens, a virtuous cycle of reforms is established.

Understanding such dynamics is operationally useful because it helps craft a long-term reform program with appropriate sequencing between short- and long-term actions. The sequencing depends on country contexts. Thus, a reform program may initially focus on the core policy dimension of rule-based decision making and help establish the processes and practices that encourage such decision making. With these core features in place, attention may be focused in the medium-term on supporting features, such as grievance redress mechanisms and systems to restrain fraudulent behavior. In the long run, systems may be established for regular and structured dialogue with stakeholders and sharing of information with the public. This type of sequencing may be appropriate for countries whose governments are initially reluctant to open up to stakeholders and the public. Such governments may be more willing to start with technocratic solutions that promote rule-based decision making, then gradually bring in more controlled accountability features, such as grievance redress mechanisms, and much later involve the public. In more open societies, it may be possible to pursue reforms simultaneously at different levels of the aforementioned hierarchy.

Operationalizing the Privilege-Resistant Agenda

An operational agenda to help countries make private sector policymaking privilege resistant may consist of a diverse set of activities supported by a range of World Bank instruments. The first step is discussion and debate on the findings of this study in each of the countries covered. Such discussions may create a demand for more in-depth diagnostic and analytic work into one or more of the policy areas covered by this study. Such an exercise may begin by evaluating work completed in the country and identify areas where further work is required, including policy areas not covered by this study. The more in-depth analysis will help identify areas of intervention, including their packaging and sequencing.

This study may also be discussed in countries in the Middle East and North Africa that are not covered in the study. Such discussions may trigger interest in conducting similar analysis for these countries. The analysis may initially be light touch following the approach of this study, followed by more in-depth analysis along the lines mentioned earlier. Alternatively, if there is sufficient interest, the analysis may move directly to the more in-depth approach.

The diversity of policy features covered in this study suggests a wide range of operational interventions that could be integral to a privilege-resistant support program. Some critical policy actions may be supported through development policy operations, whereas others may be better supported by advisory activities, result-based operations, or investment operations. Different combinations of these instruments are also possible. Table 3.1 provides examples of such interventions mapped to different World Bank tools.

Two aspects of country programing are critical to build upon the first round of reforms and make a significant dent in privilege seeking. First is the need to take a long-term programmatic approach that uses a series of World Bank operations, such as a series of development policy operations or a mix of various World Bank tools deployed in sequence. Figure 3.1 shows an example of two policy areas covered by this study, that is, investment incentives and allocation of public land.

In this example, analytic work and policy dialogue identify investment incentives and allocation of public land as priority areas to intervene

TABLE 3.1

World Bank Instruments and Operational Interventions in Support of Privilege-Resistant Policy Making

Policy area	DPO prior action	Program for results Disbursement-linked indicators	Investment project component	Advisory project component
Policy formulation process	Policy on regulatory impact assessments announced	Notice and comment system established	Funding for automation of notice and comment system	Capacity building on regulatory impact assessments
Trade and customs	Customs code made publicly available Trade clearing procedures and formalities are made publicly available	Formal appeals mechanism is established for customs-related grievances	Funding for electronic processing of customs declarations	Support to reform trade clearing procedures
Public procurement	Public procurement policy announced with defined, regulated procedure for public opening of tenders	Public procurement regulatory framework is established that provides for independent review of procurement decisions		Support to develop a public procurement regulatory framework
Allocation of land	Transparent process for allocation of public land announced	Independent body is established to which applicants for land can appeal	Funding for an automated land allocation process	Support to develop a database on available public land
Investment incentives	Clear criteria established for award of investment incentives	Database on existing investment incentives prepared		Support to carry out economic analysis of investment incentives

(continued on next page)

TABLE 3.1

World Bank Instruments and Operational Interventions in Support of Privilege-Resistant Policy Making *Continued*

Policy area	DPO prior action	Program for results Disbursement-linked indicators	Investment project component	Advisory project component
Business regulation	New law or policy enacted stipulating risk-based inspections of businesses	Automated construction permitting system is operational	Funding an automated construction permitting system Funding an automated business registry	Support to develop a risk-based system for tax inspections
Competition policy	Fully fledged competition policy and legal framework is enacted, applicable to all sectors and economic agents, with provision for institutional setup	Competition agency is provided independence from political process (specific indicators to be defined to reflect independence)	Finances provided for operations of competition agency for a defined period	Capacity building support to competition agency
Public accountability mechanisms	Establish, independent auditor, scope of mandate, freedom of information			Capacity building and advisory services to reform implementation

Note: DPO = Development Policy Operation.

FIGURE 3.1

Operationalizing the Privilege Agenda

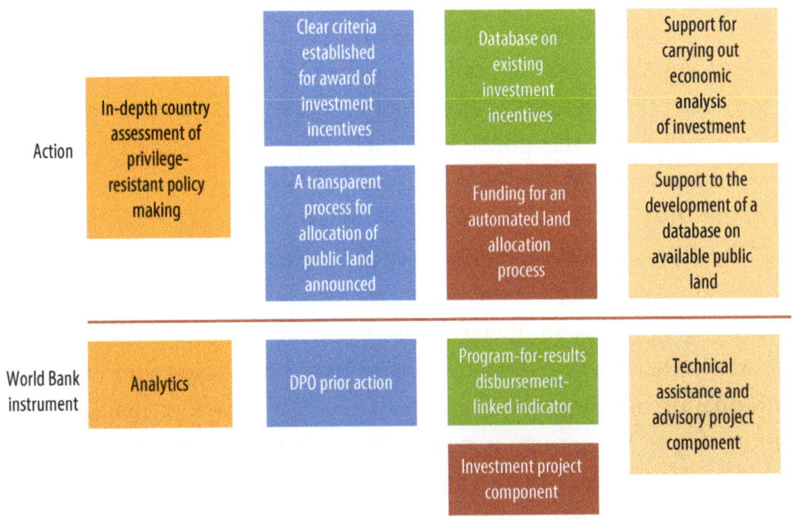

Note: DPO = Development Policy Operations.

because they are vulnerable to privilege seeking and government has shown some interest to initiate reforms in the areas. A series of reforms are programmed for each policy area. Thus, establishing clear criteria for award of investment incentives is identified as a priority reform, and this is made a prior action for a development policy operation.

The objective is to introduce the discipline of rule-based decision making, and a development policy operation (DPO) instrument is used to create the pressure for enacting the reform. A second reform is creating a database on investment to increase transparency and make it easier to assess whether the criteria for awarding incentives are being adhered to. This may be supported through a program-for-results operation. Since a database may have varying degrees of coverage and it may be difficult to achieve full coverage initially, progressive expansion of the coverage may be part of the program-for-results operation with disbursement-linked targets set for different years. Another initiative that may introduce further discipline in the investment incentives regime is economic analysis of incentives. This will help reveal whether the incentives produce their intended results. The economic analysis may be supported by an advisory operation and may follow the completion of the database.

Second is the need to exploit synergy across various parts of the World Bank. The policy areas discussed in this book do not fall in the domain of a single global practice. The field is further broadened when considering the enabling areas, such as transparency, public accountability mechanisms, and political engagement by citizens. Thus, in the aforementioned example, a second area of reform is covered as well; this is allocation of public land. Here, too a set of instruments are deployed to support a series of reforms starting with the policy announcement of a transparent process for allocation of public land, followed by the establishment of an automated land allocation process and the development of a database on available public land, each supported by lending and advisory instruments. As may be noted, the two policy areas covered by this example, that is, investment incentives and allocation of public land, both involve the award of certain privileges to businesses. Reforms in these policy areas thus share some commonalities such as establishing a clear criteria and process for giving the awards, maintaining a database on the awards so that privilege-seeking behavior may be detected, and sharing of information so that pressures are created against the seeking and granting of privileges. Thus, there is synergy between reform programs in these areas, and covering both such areas in a comprehensive program will help exploit such synergy.

To conclude, although it is challenging to address the problem of policy capture and privilege seeking, many technical solutions exist that may be political feasible. A well-sequenced set of a critical mass of such reforms may have a cumulative effect over time and create a dent in a privilege-ridden system. Many instruments are available to support such reforms in a programmatic manner and exploit synergy between different policy areas. This book may facilitate such programmatic exercises by building awareness in countries of the vulnerabilities that exist in their policy areas to privilege seeking and providing methods to assess reform opportunities and prioritize them.

Note

1. In a classic scenario, the policy and legal framework comes first, followed by the specific processes and systems that the framework is supposed to underpin. However, in the real world, reforms sometimes follow an idiosyncratic, opportunistic path and is initiated in the middle—rather than the beginning—of a stylized linear sequence.

APPENDIX A

Questionnaires to Assess the Privilege-Resistance of Different Policy Areas

TABLE A.1

Privilege-Resistant Trade and Customs Questionnaire

Privilege-Resistant Trade and Customs Questionnaire		Yes	No	How Many, Comments, Details, Sources
Tariffs structure and transparency				
1	Are tariff data publicly available on a web portal accessible to all?			
2	Is the information current, reflecting <applicable year> tariff data?			
3	How many tariff bands are there?			
4	What are the 5 highest tariff peak rates? And for which types of goods?			
Import restrictions and special regimes				
5	Are there nonautomatic import licenses, outside usual prohibited/regulated goods (for example, weapons)?			
6.1	Are the criteria for the awarding of import licenses stated in a web portal (accessible to all)?			
6.2	Are there "de facto" hidden, informal requirements, in addition to the official ones?			
7	What is the number of customs regimes?			
8	How many types of import licenses and permits exist?			
9	What is the percentage of physical inspections (%)?			
10	Does the count of physical inspections include the empty containers in the denominator? (optional)			
11	Do ex post controls exist?			
Electronic processing of declarations and connectivity				
13	Are customs declarations electronically processed for imports—at least at the main ports?			
14	If yes, are paper declarations required in addition to the electronic process?			
15	Are trade clearing procedures and formalities publicly available on a web portal?			
16	Are the main customs offices on the borders electronically connected to the headquarters? (that is, centralized book keeping, communication channels, networked database)			
Fines				
17	What is the ratio of the total value of "infringement / value of duties" for a year? (optional)			
18	Is there a publicly available web portal with the scale of infringement fines?			
19.1	Are there financial incentives for customs officials to discover fraud?			
19.2	If yes, what are the incentives for customs agents to discover fraud? No incentive; a flat incentive; a percentage of the fine; is it capped?			
19.3	Is the incentive to discover fraud capped?			
20	What is the value of the ratio "average salary / average value of the duties" of custom agents? (optional)			

(continued on next page)

TABLE A.1

Privilege-Resistant Trade and Customs Questionnaire *Continued*

Privilege-Resistant Trade and Customs Questionnaire		Yes	No	How Many, Comments, Details, Sources
Brokers				
21	Is it mandatory to hire custom brokers?			
22	What is the percentage of market share of the 5 largest brokers countrywide?			
23	What is the number of brokers' license removal (revocation) per year, over the past 5 years? (optional)			
24	When was the last time a broker's license was removed? (optional)			
25	Was there a broker's license removal in the past 5 years?			
Customs procedures and ethics				
26	Is there a procedures manual for customs agents?			
27	In the customs authority, are there internal audits regarding compliance with internal procedures?			
28	In the customs authority, are there internal audits regarding internal fraud and corruption?			
29	Is there a code of conduct or rules on conflict of interest in customs? (Please specify which one exists in comments section.)			
30	Is the customs code publicly available?			
31	Do regulations to implement the customs code exist?			
32	How many customs agents are sanctioned for corruption every year (on average over the past 5 years)? (optional)			
33	Were there custom agents sanctioned in the past year? How many?			
Laws and appeals				
34	By regulation, is there a possibility to appeal decisions?			
35	By regulation, is there an official time frame for appeal?			
36	By regulation, is there a possibility of recourse to independent jurisdiction in the final instance?			
37	How many appeal cases are there per year (please average over the past 5 years)? (optional)			

TABLE A.2

Privilege-Resistant Procurement Questionnaire

Privilege-Resistant Procurement Questionnaire		Yes	No	Comments, Details
Institutional and regulatory frameworks				
1.1	Is there a regulatory body or an authority that oversees public procurement?			
1.2	If there is a regulatory body or an authority in charge of public procurement; does it have its own budget?			
1.3.1	Pursuant to the regulatory framework, is the regulatory body's involvement in direct procurement operations prohibited?			
1.3.2	Pursuant to the regulatory framework, is the regulatory body's involvement in procurement planning prohibited?			
1.3.3	Pursuant to the regulatory framework, is the regulatory body's involvement in bids evaluation prohibited?			
1.3.4	In practice, is the regulatory body's involvement in direct procurement operations prohibited?			
1.3.5	In practice, is the regulatory body's involvement in procurement planning prohibited?			
1.3.6	In practice, is the regulatory body's involvement in bids evaluation prohibited?			
2.1	Is there a regular procurement planning exercise instituted by law or regulation that starts with the preparation of multiyear plans for the government agencies, from which annual operating plans are derived?			
2.2	Are procurement plans prepared in support of the budget planning and formulation process?			
Fair opportunity				
3.1	Does the regulatory framework require that procurement opportunities other than sole source or price quotations be publicly advertised in a national gazette or widely distributed newspaper?			
3.2	Does the regulatory framework require that procurement opportunities other than sole source or price quotations be publicly advertised in a central web portal?			
4	Does the legal framework establish that participation of any contractor, supplier or group of suppliers, or contractors is based on qualification?			
5.1	Does the regulatory framework establish rules that favor national companies?			
5.2	What is the margin of preference for national suppliers?			
6.1	Is it mandatory to enroll as a supplier on a national suppliers' registry to participate in biddings?			
6.2	Is the registration time frame specified in the legal framework?			
7	Is there a classification system for the firms / contractors?			
8.1	Does the regulatory framework provide a list of qualification criteria that suppliers must meet in order to be admitted to submit a bid?			
8.2	Does the regulatory framework provide that qualification criteria should be communicated to suppliers, either through the tender notice or tender documents?			
9	Does the legal framework establish rules that favor state-owned enterprises?			
10.1	Does the regulatory framework and its implementing regulations provide procedures and methodologies for assessment of technical capacity?			

(continued on next page)

TABLE A.2

Privilege-Resistant Procurement Questionnaire *Continued*

Privilege-Resistant Procurement Questionnaire		Yes	No	Comments, Details
10.2	Does the regulatory framework and its implementing regulations provide procedures and methodologies for combining price and technical capacity under different circumstances?			
Transparency, confidentiality, and access to information				
11	Does the legal framework mandate the following? Check all that apply.			
11.1.1	By regulation, opening of tenders follows a defined and regulated procedure.			
11.1.2	Public opening of tenders occurs in the 24 hours following the closing date for bid submission.			
11.2.1	By regulation, records of proceedings for bid openings are retained.			
11.2.2	By regulation, records of proceedings for bid openings are available for review.			
11.3	By regulation, security and confidentiality of bids are maintained prior to bid opening.			
11.4	By regulation, disclosure of specific sensitive information during debriefing or clarifications is prohibited.			
12.1	Is there an integrated information system that provides, at a minimum, up-to-date procurement information, including tender invitations, requests for proposals?			
12.2	Is there an integrated information system that provides, at a minimum, up-to-date procurement information, including contract award information?			
13	Is this information system accessible to the public at no or minimum cost? (Please specify the cost.)			
14	Are the following decisions publicly posted on a government website or a national gazette? Check all that apply.			
14.1	Modifications of tender documents			
14.2	Cancellation of a call for tenders			
14.3	Award notices			
Grievance, complaint, recourse				
15.1	Does the regulatory framework provide for the right of participants to ask for an independent review in a procurement process?			
15.2	Does the regulatory framework establish time frames for issuance of decisions by the procuring agency?			
15.3	Does the regulatory framework establish time frames for issuance of decisions by the administrative review body?			
15.4	Is the administrative review body institutionally independent and autonomous with regard to resolving complaints?			
Integrity and accountability				
16.1	Does the regulatory framework for procurement include provisions addressing the following?			
16.2	The regulatory framework for procurement gives instructions on how to incorporate fraud, corruption, conflict of interest, and unethical behavior in tendering documents.			
17	Does the regulatory framework cover the following? Check all that apply.			
17.1	Covers fraud and corruption.			

(continued on next page)

TABLE A.2

Privilege-Resistant Procurement Questionnaire *Continued*

Privilege-Resistant Procurement Questionnaire		Yes	No	Comments, Details
17.2	Provides a definition of what is considered fraud and corruption.			
17.3	Spells out the individual responsibilities and consequences for government employees found guilty of fraud or corruption in procurement.			
17.4	Spells out the individual responsibilities and consequences for private firms or individuals found guilty of fraud or corruption in procurement.			
18	Is there a secure, accessible, and confidential system for the public reporting of cases of fraud, unethical behavior, and corruption?			
19	Does the regulatory framework provide for the following? Check all that apply.			
19.1	Exclusions for criminal or corrupt activities.			
19.2	Administrative debarment under the law subject to due process.			
19.3	Prohibition of commercial relations or black listing.			
20	Does the government have in place an anticorruption program to the following? Check all that apply.			
20.1	Prevent corruption in public procurement.			
20.2	Detect corruption in public procurement.			

TABLE A.3

Privilege-Resistant Competition Policy Questionnaire

Privilege-Resistant Competition Policy Questionnaire	Yes	No	Number, Figure, Score, Comments	Who Will Respond	Source
1.1. Is there a competition act/law in place?			Provide the complete name and number of the act/law.	Competition authorities or their equivalent in the ministries	
If the answer is yes, when was it enacted (mm/dd/yyyy)?					
1.1.1. Is there a draft bill with Parliament or with other segments of government?					
1.2. Is there a functional competition authority in place? By functional we mean an authority with executive regulations in place (to activate the law), staff, and a budget. If the answer is yes:					
a) Please provide the full name of the competition authority.			Provide the complete name of the relevant authority.		
b) If available, please provide the website for the competition authority.			Provide the website address of the relevant authority.		
c) If a specific act or law for the creation of the agency is needed, when was such act or law issued (mm/yyyy)?			Provide the complete name and number of the act/law.		

(continued on next page)

TABLE A.3

Privilege-Resistant Competition Policy Questionnaire *Continued*

Privilege-Resistant Competition Policy Questionnaire	Yes	No	Number, Figure, Score, Comments	Who Will Respond	Source
d) Where relevant, what is the parent ministry that hosts the competition authority?					
e) When did the competition authority start to take on casework (mm/yyyy)?					
Scope of the competition framework					
2.1. The legal competition framework has explicit provisions to address the following (check all that apply):					
a) Vertical restraints / agreements					
b) Abuse of dominance					
c) Merger control					
d) Anticompetitive regulation / competition advocacy					
e) Anticompetitive actions of state and public bodies					
f) Actions of public officials that facilitate anticompetitive behavior					
g) Other (for example, consumer protection, state aid control, unfair competition, procurement). Please specify in the comments section.					
2.2. The legal competition framework does not apply to the following (check all that apply and specify in comments section):					
a) State-owned enterprises (in general or in particular sectors)					
b) Other state bodies and government agencies (in general or in particular sectors)					
c) Certain sectors of the economy					
d) Certain goods or services					
e) Legal monopolies					
f) Professional associations					
g) Conduct that is required or authorized by other government authority (in addition to exclusion that might apply to whole sectors or markets					
2.3. Please indicate which of the following are stated objectives of your country's competition policy:					
a) Ensuring effective competitive process					
b) Promoting consumer welfare					
c) Enhancing efficiency					
d) Ensuring economic freedom					
e) Ensuring a level playing field for small and medium enterprises					

(continued on next page)

TABLE A.3

Privilege-Resistant Competition Policy Questionnaire *Continued*

Privilege-Resistant Competition Policy Questionnaire	Yes	No	Number, Figure, Score, Comments	Who Will Respond	Source
f) Promoting fairness and equality					
g) Reducing poverty					
h) Promoting consumer choice					
i) Achieving market integration					
j) Facilitating privatization and market liberalization					
k) Promoting competitiveness in international markets					
l) Other. Please specify in the comments section.					
2.4. Does the competition framework contain a framework for exemptions to restrictive practices (for example, price fixing, market allocation, coordination of production)?			If yes, what are the possible justifications for exemptions?		
2.5. Can an anticompetitive merger or acquisition be allowed on grounds other than competition (for example, public interest)?			If yes, please explain under which grounds and provide examples of such merger cases handled by the authority		
State aid and subsidy control 3.1. Is there a specific framework and procedure that public bodies should follow to grant state aid (subsidies, tax breaks, government land, concessional loans) to private and state-owned enterprises?					
3.2. If there are general or sectoral criteria to grant state aid (for example, subsidies, tax breaks, concessional loans), do they include an assessment on market competition?					
3.3. Is there a registry of state aid (for example, subsidies, tax breaks, government land, concessional loans) granted by the government to private and state-owned enterprises?					
Institutional setup 4.1. The government body that is responsible for the enforcement of competition law is the following (check all options that apply and explain in the comments section):					
a) Independent body					
b) Government department with a ministry					
c) Public prosecutor					
d) Sector-specific regulator					
e) Specialized tribunal					

(continued on next page)

TABLE A.3

Privilege-Resistant Competition Policy Questionnaire *Continued*

Privilege-Resistant Competition Policy Questionnaire	Yes	No	Number, Figure, Score, Comments	Who Will Respond	Source
f) Other					
4.2. The competition authority is accountable to the following:					
a) Government minister. Please specify in the comments section.					
b) Government department. Please specify in the comments section.					
c) Parliament					
d) Other. Please specify in the comments section.					
4.3. Members of the competition authority (commissioner, chairman, director) are appointed by the following:					
a) President or prime minister					
b) Minister					
c) President or prime minister with consent of Congress or Parliament					
d) Congress or Parliament					
e) Representatives of entrepreneurial or consumer associations, or academics					
f) Judicial system					
g) Other. Please specify in the comments section.					
4.4. Can the competition authority's decisions be vetoed by the line ministry(ies) or any other body of the executive branch? Please specify in the comments section.					
4.5. Who allocates the budget of the competition authority (for example, parliament, government, self-financing through merger filing fees or fines, other)?					
4.6. Is the competition authority governed by a single chairman or a collegiate body?					
4.7. How long is the term of office of the agency's board members?					
4.7.1. If it is a fixed-term appointment, is it renewable?					
4.8. Are board members jointly nominated or at intervals (term of board members' mandates does not coincide) so as to ensure continuity in operations and strategy implementation?					
4.9. Are market operators represented in the board of the competition authority?					

(continued on next page)

TABLE A.3

Privilege-Resistant Competition Policy Questionnaire *Continued*

Privilege-Resistant Competition Policy Questionnaire	Yes	No	Number, Figure, Score, Comments	Who Will Respond	Source
4.10. May the competition authority board members hold other offices or appointments in the government or the industry?					
4.11. How long is the term of office of the agency board members?					
4.12. How can the board members be dismissed from office? Please specify in the comments section.					
4.13. Is there a fixed period during which removal is prohibited?					
4.14. Is there a cooling-off period during which board members and staff of the competition authority cannot take jobs in the government or companies investigated after their term of office/employment contract? Please specify in the comments section.					
Interaction with other government policies and advocacy with government agencies					
5.1. Do sector-specific regulators have a competition law mandate, including the investigation of anticompetitive practices or the analysis of mergers? Can the staff of the regulator participate in the investigations and market inquiries carried out by the competition authority? Please specify in the comments section.					
a) Telecommunications regulator					
b) Energy regulator					
c) Transport regulator					
d) Banking regulator					
e) Public procurement agency					
f) Consumer protection agency					
g) Other. Please specify in the comments section.					
5.2. Does the competition authority have the mandate to issue opinions on government policies, draft legislation, and regulations as part of its role in advocacy?					
5.2.1. If the answer is yes, are the opinions binding?					
5.2.2. If the opinions are not binding, is there a mechanism to monitor the implementation of the competition authority's opinions?					
5.3. Has the competition authority signed protocols or memoranda of understanding with other government bodies? If the answer is yes, with which bodies? Check all that apply.					

(continued on next page)

TABLE A.3

Privilege-Resistant Competition Policy Questionnaire *Continued*

Privilege-Resistant Competition Policy Questionnaire	Yes	No	Number, Figure, Score, Comments	Who Will Respond	Source
a) Telecommunications regulator					
b) Energy regulator					
c) Transport regulator					
d) Banking regulator					
e) Public procurement agency					
f) Consumer protection agency					
g) Other. Please specify in the comments section.					
5.4. Does the regulator have the power to define and recruit its staff? If not, is it dependent on the staff of a particular ministry?					
Powers of the authority					
6.1. The competition authority may initiate an investigation in the following circumstances (check all that apply):					
a) Once it has received a complaint or request from the public					
b) After conducting its own research or market enquiry					
c) At the request or recommendation of a government minister					
d) After a request or recommendation from another authority					
e) Other. Please specify in the comments section.					
6.2. The competition authority has the power to gather information through the following (check all that apply):					
a) Requesting parties to voluntarily provide information					
b) Issuing a summons or subpoena					
c) Conducting unannounced raids (search and seizure) and inspections					
d) Market studies					
e) Other. Please specify in the comments section.					
6.3. Does the competition authority have the necessary power and tools to uncover illegal practices (for example, case prioritization, adequate fines, leniency program,[a] inspection powers)?			Please explain any limitations faced by the authority, or what tools and powers have been particularly useful to uncover illegal practices.		

(continued on next page)

TABLE A.3

Privilege-Resistant Competition Policy Questionnaire *Continued*

Privilege-Resistant Competition Policy Questionnaire	Yes	No	Number, Figure, Score, Comments	Who Will Respond	Source
Due process					
7.1. Does the competition authority publish guidelines / communications/updates explaining how the following are assessed (check all that apply)?					
a) Horizontal agreement					
b) Vertical restraints					
c) Abuse of dominance					
d) Merger control					
e) Fine setting					
f) Investigative procedures					
g) Treatment of confidential information					
7.2. Does your legislation allow for competition authority decisions to be effectively reviewed by an independent appellate body? Please explain in the comments section.					
7.3. Does your competition law provide for a fair and transparent process to the parties involved in competition investigations and proceedings and for effective judicial review? If yes, indicate what instruments are provided by your legislation (check all that apply).			Please explain how the listed instruments are used.		
a) Oral hearings					
b) Technical discussions with case handlers					
c) Access to nonconfidential version of statement of objections to be informed about the reasons for the investigation					
d) Access to the case files					
e) Annual reports					
f) Publication of reasoned decisions					
g) Other instruments to provide for the right of defense. Please specify in the comments section.					
7.4. Are there protections for ensuring that confidential or privileged business information provided by companies during investigations, merger reviews, and market studies that are not disclosed to third parties?					
7.4.1. Can the parties appeal decisions granting access to confidential information before the courts? If so, does this appeal have a suspensive effect?					
7.5. Are there different teams from the competition authority/(ies) involved in opening the investigation, prosecuting, and reaching a decision?			If the answer is yes, provide information about the separation of functions.		

(continued on next page)

TABLE A.3

Privilege-Resistant Competition Policy Questionnaire *Continued*

Privilege-Resistant Competition Policy Questionnaire	Yes	No	Number, Figure, Score, Comments	Who Will Respond	Source
7.6. Is the status of the competition authority staff the same as that of civil servants? If yes, do general administrative rules on matters such as conflict of interest apply to the staff of the competition authority?					
7.6.1. If the answer is no, are there specific rules to avoid conflict of interest of case handlers and members of the decision body?					
Operational indicators					
8.1. Number of technical staff working in the agency and dealing with competition matters?					
a) Number of lawyers?					
b) Number of economists?					
c) Number of staff with postgraduate degree (master's or doctorate)?					
8.2. Number of competition authority's decisions appealed in the last 3 years?					
8.3. Number of decisions upheld and rejected by the courts?					
8.4. Number of agency's opinions on laws, regulations, and other government decisions in the last 2 calendar years?			Please, in addition, specify the main opinions (with larger impact).		
8.5. Number of sector inquiries carried out in the last 2 years? Please specify which sectors, where relevant.					
8.6. Agency's budget in the last fiscal year (in local currency)?					
8.7. Amount of fines imposed in the last fiscal year (in local currency)?					

a. Partial or total exoneration from the penalties that would otherwise be applicable to a cartel member that reports its cartel membership to a competition enforcement agency.

TABLE A.4

Privilege-Resistant Incentives Policy Questionnaire

Privilege-Resistant Incentives Policy Questionnaire		Yes	No	Comment, Data Source
1	Does the government have an incentives policy that clearly and publicly states the objectives of the incentives regime?			
2	Does the incentives policy include statements related to the following (check all that apply):			
2.1	The government review process of the incentive policy/regime			
2.2	The reform/change process of the incentive policy/regime			
2.3	The publication of information on incentives offered			
2.4	The principles of the awarding process of incentives			
3	Does the government perform a regular review of the relevance and appropriateness of the incentives policy in pursuing its investment policy objectives?			
4	Does the government make the results of the review available to the public?			
5	Does the government on a regular basis conduct an assessment of the fiscal cost associated with the incentives regime (tax expenditure statement and cost of financial incentives statement)?			
6	Does the government make the results of this assessment available to the public?			
Consultations				
7	De jure: Does the law require consultation at the time of formulation of the relevant laws, regulations, and decrees relating to incentives?			
8	De facto: Is an interested / affected investor given an opportunity to comment on the relevant laws, regulations, and decrees relating to incentives prior to their finalization?			
9	When changes to the incentive regime are introduced, are the proposed changes formally communicated to the public before such changes are adopted?			
Administration and governance of incentives				
10	Is there a specific authority in charge of the administration and awarding of incentives to firms? Please describe in the comments section.			
11	During the awarding process of incentives, are incentives granted automatically to investors?			
11.1	During the awarding process of incentives, are incentives granted based on a review or screening process by the authority(ies) in charge of incentive administration?			
11.2	If awarded based on review/screening process, is it based on a list of criteria published in advance?			
11.3	Are these criteria available to the public on a web portal or a national gazette?			
12	De jure: Does the law require the investor to be appropriately notified of any specific decision on incentives taken by the administrating authority of incentives?			
13	De facto: Is the affected investor appropriately notified of any specific decision on incentives taken by the administrative authority?			
14	When a positive decision is rendered granting some incentives to the investor, is the decision published?			

(continued on next page)

TABLE A.4

Privilege-Resistant Incentives Policy Questionnaire *Continued*

Privilege-Resistant Incentives Policy Questionnaire		Yes	No	Comment, Data Source
15	When a negative decision is rendered (refusal to grant all or some of the incentives requested by the investor), does the law require that the decision be communicated in writing and motivated (meaning that the implementing body has to provide some form of justification for the negative decision) to the investor?			
16	De jure: Does the law allow the affected investor to appeal to a higher authority once a decision has been taken based on the application on incentives by the administrating authority?			
17	De facto: Does the investor get an opportunity to appeal to a higher authority once a decision is taken based on the application on incentives?			
Transparency and access to information				
18	De jure: Does the law require publication of relevant laws, regulations, and decrees relating to incentives?			
19	De facto: Are relevant laws, regulations, and decrees relating to incentives easily and publicly accessible in practice (for example, through a government gazette or online)?			
20	De jure: Does the law mandate that the government maintain and publish an inventory of investment incentives that lists the types of incentives available to investors?			
21	De facto: Does the government maintain a central database / inventory of investment incentives that provides a comprehensive list of incentives offered to investors?			
22	Is the inventory published in a source that is available to the public?			
23	Does the central database / inventory include the categories of information listed below (check all that apply):			
23.1	Overview information on incentives, including a short description, overarching objectives, type / form (for example, tax holiday, matching grant), maximum value / benefit for investors, and their legal base			
23.2	Information to apply for incentives, including eligibility criteria, awarding authority, required documentation, procedures, and timelines			
22.3	Information on appeal procedures, as well as monitoring and performance management procedures			
23.4	Information on further resources, including direct links to other official web pages, or contact information for any questions / follow-up relating to the application and awarding process of incentives			
23.5	Information about incentives awarded in the past, including budgeted and awarded funds per year, as well as the number of beneficiaries			

TABLE A.5

Privilege-Resistant Access to Public Industrial Land Questionnaire

Privilege-Resistant Access to Public Industrial Land Questionnaire		Yes	No	Comment
Institutional and regulatory framework for public industrial land				
1	Is there a public industrial land allocation system in the country?			
2	Is the management responsibility over public industrial land unambiguously assigned to a dedicated authority who has a clear mandate?			
2a	If yes, is the industrial land authority independent?			
2b	If yes, does the industrial land authority have adequate budgets and human resources that ensure responsible management of public industrial lands?			
3	Is public industrial land allocated to the private sector though auctions or tenders?			
4	Is public industrial land allocated to the private sector after a cost-benefit or business plan analysis?			
5	Is public industrial land allocated to the private sector after a due diligence process?			
6	Is public industrial land allocated at market prices in a transparent process irrespective of the investor's status (for example, domestic or foreign)?			
7	In practice, can public land categories be changed easily, providing for windfalls? (for example, allocating land as agricultural land at low prices, then changing to construction land) Please provide typical stories in the comments section.			
8	Is the assessment of land values for tax purposes based on market prices?			
Transparency, publicity, and scrutiny				
9	Is the land authority required by law or regulation to publish a report of allocated public industrial land every year?			
10	De facto, does the land authority publish a report of allocated public industrial land every year?			
11	Is this report available to the public either on a web portal or in a national gazette?			
12	By regulation, is all the information on the public industrial land inventory accessible to the public on a web portal or national Gazette?			
13	De facto, is all the information on the public industrial land inventory accessible to the public? (web portal or national gazette)			
14	By regulation, are valuation rolls of public industrial land publicly accessible? (web portal or national gazette)			
15	De facto: Are valuation rolls of public industrial land publicly accessible? (web portal or national gazette)			
16	Are valuation rolls regularly updated?			
17	Is public industrial land clearly inventoried and identified on the ground or on maps?			
18	Is all privately held land formally mapped?			
19	Is all privately held land formally registered in the cadaster?			
20	Can records in the registry be searched by both right-holder name and parcel?			
21	Is most ownership information in the registry or cadaster current?			
22	Can copies or extracts of documents recording rights in property be obtained by anyone who pays the necessary formal fee, if any?			

(continued on next page)

TABLE A.5

Privilege-Resistant Access to Public Industrial Land Questionnaire *Continued*

Privilege-Resistant Access to Public Industrial Land Questionnaire		Yes	No	Comment
Grievance and recourse				
23	By regulation, does the industrial land authority provide arguments and explanations when it renders a negative decision?			
24	By regulation, is it possible to appeal a negative land allocation decision?			
25	Is there an independent body to which applicants can appeal against the decision of the industrial land authority?			
26	By regulation, is the appeal committee required to render a decision within a specific timeframe?			
Enforcement: tax collection				
27	Are all property holders liable for land tax and listed on the tax roll?			
28	Are there exemptions to the payment of land and property taxes?			
29	Are the exemptions that exist based on clear and publicized criteria and applied in a transparent and consistent manner?			

Note: This questionnaire can be applied to land for commercial, real estate, or tourism purposes.

TABLE A.6

Privilege-Resistant Access to Finance Questionnaire

Privilege-Resistant Access to Finance Questionnaire		Yes	No	Figure, Details
Related parties and politically exposed persons				
1	Is there a central bank regulation (or a regulation from the banking supervision authority) regarding lending to related parties?			
2	Does the definition of "related parties" include shareholders as individuals?			
3	Does the definition of "related parties" include shareholders as firms?			
4	Do related parties include shareholders' relatives in the first degree (spouse, parents, brothers and sisters, and children)?			
5	Do related parties include shareholders' relatives in the second degree (in-laws, nephews, nieces, cousins)?			
6.1	By regulation, do banks have policies and processes to identify individual exposures to and transactions with related parties?			
6.2	If yes, does this include the total amount of exposure?			
6.3	If yes, are these transactions monitored and reported through an independent credit review or audit process?			
7	Does the central bank impose that banks have policies and processes to prevent persons benefiting from the transaction or persons related to such a person from being part of the process of granting and managing the transaction?			
8	Is it common practice that banks' board members with conflicts of interest are excluded from the approval process of granting and managing related party transactions?			

(continued on next page)

TABLE A.6

Privilege-Resistant Access to Finance Questionnaire *Continued*

Privilege-Resistant Access to Finance Questionnaire		Yes	No	Figure, Details
9	Are operations (new credits, credit extension, total and partial write-offs, rescheduling, guarantees, off-balance sheet operations) to related parties subject to prior approval by banks' boards?			
10	In particular, are write-offs of related-party exposures exceeding specified amounts, or otherwise posing special risks, subject to prior approval by banks' boards?			
11.1	Is lending to related parties monitored through onsite supervision, such as audits?			
11.2	What is the frequency for these audits to be performed?			
12	Is lending to related parties monitored through off-site supervision from the central bank?			
13	Are there mechanisms to limit exposure to related parties: for instance, to deduct such exposures from capital when assessing capital adequacy or to require collateralization of such exposures?			
14	By regulation, do banks apply the GAFI-FATF principles regarding politically exposed persons?			
15	Does the government or the central bank publish a list of politically exposed persons?			
16	By regulation, is there an enhanced due diligence on politically exposed persons (including, among other things, escalation to the bank's senior management level of decisions on entering into business relationships with these persons)?			
17	Are there clear rules on what records regarding politically exposed persons must be kept and their retention period?			
18	Do central banks audit banks regarding politically exposed persons?			
Corporate governance				
19.1	By regulation, are large loans overseen by the state-owned banks' boards?			
19.2	By regulation, are large loans overseen by the state-owned private banks' boards?			
20	Are there independent administrators in state-owned banks' boards?			
21	By regulation, are there independent administrators in private banks' boards?			
22	By regulation, are there rules imposing the existence of a board-level audit committee?			
23	If yes, by regulation, is the audit committee chaired by an independent administrator?			
24	By regulation, does the internal audit function fully report to the audit committee?			
Insider trading				
25	By regulation, are there rules to prevent insider trading?			
26	By regulation, are there rules to sanction insider trading?			
27	By regulation, is there an agency responsible for enforcing insider trading regulations?			
27	Does the capital markets authority enforce regulation through on-site inspections?			
28	Does the capital markets authority enforce regulation through off-site inspections?			

(continued on next page)

TABLE A.6

Privilege-Resistant Access to Finance Questionnaire *Continued*

Privilege-Resistant Access to Finance Questionnaire		Yes	No	Figure, Details
Effectiveness of sanctions				
29	What were the 5 last sanctions imposed by the central bank regarding money laundering? Please specify the years, type of sanction and the amount of the fine.			
30	What were the 5 last sanctions imposed by the central bank regarding internal control? Please specify the years, type of sanction and the amount of the fine.			
31	What were the 5 last sanctions imposed by the central bank regarding money-related parties? Please specify the years, type of sanction and the amount of the fine.			

TABLE A.7

Privilege-Resistant Business Regulation Questionnaire

Privilege-Resistant Business Regulation Questionnaire	Yes	No	Comments
Business registration			
A.1. By regulation, are the "requirements" for obtaining business registration specified on a web portal or at the regulator's office? Please specify where in the comments section.			
A.2. By regulation, are the "fees" for obtaining business registration specified on a web portal or at the regulator's office Please specify where in the comments section.			
A.3. By regulation, are the "procedures" for obtaining business registration specified on a web portal or at the regulator's office? Please specify where in the comments section.			
A.4. By regulation, registration is one-off and does not need to be renewed periodically.			
A.5. Are there informal requirements for obtaining business registration, in addition to the official ones?			
A.6. Are there hidden, informal fees for obtaining business registration, in addition to the official ones?			
A.7. Are there hidden, informal steps for obtaining business registration, in addition to the official ones?			
Permits and licenses: construction permits			
B.1. By regulation, are the requirements for obtaining construction permits publicly available on a website or national gazette? Please specify where in the comments section.			
B.2. By regulation, are the fees for obtaining construction permits publicly available on a website or national gazette? Please specify where in the comments section.			
B.3. By regulation, are the procedures for obtaining construction permits publicly available on a website or national gazette? Please specify where in the comments section.			
B.4. Are there hidden requirements for obtaining construction permits in addition to the official ones?			
B.5. Are there hidden fees for obtaining construction permits in addition to the official ones?			
B.6. Are there hidden procedures for obtaining construction permits in addition to the official ones?			
B.7. By regulation, does obtaining construction permits first require a number of other preapprovals?			
B.7. In practice, does obtaining construction permits first require a number of other preapprovals?			
B.8. By regulation, do construction permits need to be renewed periodically?			
B.9. By regulation, are the relevant agencies required to inform applicants about decisions or delays in providing construction permits within a specified timeframe?			

(continued on next page)

TABLE A.7

Privilege-Resistant Business Regulation Questionnaire *Continued*

Privilege-Resistant Business Regulation Questionnaire	Yes	No	Comments
B.10. In practice, do the relevant agencies inform applicants about decisions or delays in providing construction permits within a specified timeframe?			
B.11. By law or regulation, are the relevant agencies required to provide justification for negative decisions or delays?			
B.12. In practice, are the relevant agencies required to provide justification for negative decisions or delays?			
B.13. By regulation, are there appeal mechanisms? Please describe them in the comments section.			
B.14. In practice, are appeal mechanisms used and effective? Please describe them in the comments section.			
Tax inspections			
C.1. By regulation, do the authorities follow risk-based approaches to planning tax inspections?			
C.2. In practice, do the authorities follow risk-based approaches to planning tax inspections?			
C.3.1. By law or regulation, routine tax inspection visits are announced.			
C3.2. The purpose of the tax inspection visit is clearly stated.			
C.4. In practice, routine tax inspection visits are announced.			
C.5. By regulation, are the tax compliance requirements published and accessible on a web portal or at the relevant authority?			
C.6. In practice, are the tax compliance requirements published and accessible on a web portal or at the relevant authority?			
C.7. By regulation, are the tax enforcement decisions vetted by a commission or supervisor, at least for major decisions (as opposed to the inspector alone)?			
C.8. By regulation, do tax inspectors / inspectorates have powers to suspend / stop operations of businesses?			
C.9. By regulation, are tax inspectors required to provide copies of inspection reports to the inspected firms within a specified time period?			
C.10. By regulation, are firms given a grace period during which they may remedy deficiencies?			
C.11. By regulation, is there a transparent, risk-based system to filter or manage complaints from the public instead of conducting additional tax inspection any time a complaint is received?			
C.12. By regulation, are there grievance reporting and redress mechanisms?			
C.13. In practice, are there grievance reporting and redress mechanisms?			

TABLE A.8

Conflict of Interest Questionnaire

Conflict of Interest Questionnaire		Yes	No	Comments
Legal framework				
1	Are there laws regulating restrictions on conflict of interest?			
2	Is there a constitutional requirement to avoid specified conflict(s) of interest?			
3	In there a code of conduct / ethics regarding conflict of interest?			

(continued on next page)

TABLE A.8

Conflict of Interest Questionnaire *Continued*

Conflict of Interest Questionnaire		Yes	No	Comments
Officials covered by regulations on conflict of interest				
5	Are head(s) of state obligated to avoid specified conflict(s) of interest?			
6	Are ministers / cabinet members obligated to avoid specified conflict(s) of interest?			
7	Are members of Parliament obligated to avoid specified conflict(s) of interest?			
8	Are civil servants obligated to avoid specified conflict(s) of interest?			
9	Are spouses and children obligated to avoid specified conflict(s) of interest?			
By regulation, are there restrictions for the following public officials regarding the following items?				
Head(s) of state				
Income and assets (check all that apply)				
10	Accepting gifts			
11	Private firm ownership or stock holdings			
12	Ownership of state-owned enterprises			
Business activities (check all that apply)				
13	Holding government contracts			
14	Board member, advisor, or company officer of private firm			
15	NGO or labor union membership			
16	Outside employment			
17	Post-employment			
Ministers / cabinet members				
Income and assets (check all that apply)				
14	Accepting gifts			
15	Private firm ownership or stock holdings			
16	Ownership of state-owned enterprises			
Business activities (check all that apply)				
17	Holding government contracts			
18	Board member, advisor, or company officer of private firm			
19	NGO or labor union membership			
20	Outside employment			
21	Postemployment			
Members of Parliament				
Income and assets (check all that apply)				
22	Accepting gifts			
23	Private firm ownership or stock holdings			
24	Ownership of state-owned enterprises			
Business activities (check all that apply)				
25	Holding government contracts			
26	Board member, advisor, or company officer of private firm			

(continued on next page)

TABLE A.8

Conflict of Interest Questionnaire *Continued*

Conflict of Interest Questionnaire		Yes	No	Comments
27	NGO or labor union membership			
28	Outside employment			
29	Post-employment			
Civil servants				
Income and assets (check all that apply)				
30	Accepting gifts			
31	Private firm ownership or stock holdings			
32	Ownership of state-owned enterprises			
Business activities (check all that apply)				
33	Holding government contracts			
34	Board member, advisor, or company officer of private firm			
35	NGO or labor union membership			
36	Outside employment			
37	Post-employment			
Spouses and children				
Income and assets (check all that apply)				
38	Accepting gifts			
39	Private firm ownership or stock holdings			
40	Ownership of state-owned enterprises			
Business activities (check all that apply)				
41	Holding government contracts			
42	Board member, advisor, or company officer of private firm			
43	NGO or labor union membership			
44	Outside employment			
45	Post-employment			
Sanctions for the following public officials				
Head(s) of state				
46	Are there penal sanctions, fines, or administrative sanctions stipulated for violations of conflict of interest regulations that restrict behavior?			
Ministers / cabinet members				
47	Are there penal sanctions, fines, or administrative sanctions stipulated for violations of conflict of interest regulations that restrict behavior?			
Members of Parliament				
48	Are there penal sanctions, fines, or administrative sanctions stipulated for violations of conflict of interest regulations that restrict behavior?			
Civil servants				
49	Are there penal sanctions, fines, or administrative sanctions stipulated for violations of conflict of interest regulations that restrict behavior?			

(continued on next page)

TABLE A.8

Conflict of Interest Questionnaire *Continued*

Conflict of Interest Questionnaire		Yes	No	Comments
Monitoring and oversight for the following public officials				
Head(s) of state (check all that apply)				
50	Is there a specific enforcement body?			
51	Is there a process for addressing potential violations of conflict of interest restrictions?			
Ministers / cabinet members (check all that apply)				
52	Is there a specific enforcement body?			
53	Is there a process for addressing potential violations of conflict of interest restrictions?			
Members of Parliament (check all that apply)				
54	Is there a specific enforcement body?			
55	Is there a process for addressing potential violations of conflict of interest restrictions?			
Civil servants (check all that apply)				
56	Is there a specific enforcement body?			
57	Is there a process for addressing potential violations of conflict of interest restrictions?			

TABLE A.9

Asset Disclosure Questionnaire

Asset Disclosure Questionnaire		Yes	No	Details	Citation
Legal Framework					
1	Are there laws regulating requirement to disclose?				
2	Is there a constitutional requirement to disclose?				
3	Is there a code of conduct / ethics for public officials?				
Are the following public officials covered by asset disclosure obligations (check all that apply)?					
4	Head of state				
5	Ministers / cabinet members				
6	Members of Parliament				
7	Civil servants				
8	Spouses and children				
Disclosure items (check all that apply)					
9	Head of state				
10	Ministers / cabinet members				
11	Members of Parliament				
12	Civil servants				
13	Spouses and children				

(continued on next page)

TABLE A.9

Asset Disclosure Questionnaire *Continued*

Asset Disclosure Questionnaire		Yes	No	Details	Citation
Filing frequency (check all that apply)					
14	Head of state				
15	Ministers / cabinet members				
16	Members of Parliament				
17	Civil servants				
Sanctions for the following public officials					
Head of state					
18	Are sanctions stipulated for nonfiling (fines, administrative, or criminal)?				
19	Are sanctions stipulated for false disclosure (fines, administrative, or criminal)?				
Ministers / cabinet members					
20	Are sanctions stipulated for nonfiling (fines, administrative, or criminal)?				
21	Are sanctions stipulated for false disclosure (fines, administrative, or criminal)?				
Members of Parliament					
22	Are sanctions stipulated for nonfiling (fines, administrative, or criminal)?				
23	Are sanctions stipulated for false disclosure (fines, administrative, or criminal)?				
Civil servants					
24	Are sanctions stipulated for nonfiling (fines, administrative, or criminal)?				
25	Are sanctions stipulated for false disclosure (fines, administrative, or criminal)?				
Monitoring and oversight					
Head of state					
26	Are enforcement, depository and verifying bodies explicitly identified?				
27	Is a process specified for resolving conflict of interest?				
Ministers / cabinet members					
28	Are enforcement, depository and verifying bodies explicitly identified?				
29	Is a process specified for resolving conflict of interest?				
Members of Parliament					
30	Are enforcement, depository, and verifying bodies explicitly identified?				
31	Is a process specified for resolving conflict of interest?				
Civil servants					
32	Are enforcement, depository, and verifying bodies explicitly identified?				
33	Is a process specified for resolving conflict of interest?				
Public access to declarations					
Head of State					
34	Is public availability specified?				
35	Is the length of records maintenance specified?				
36	Are penalties for violating nondisclosure of declarations specified?				

(continued on next page)

TABLE A.9

Asset Disclosure Questionnaire *Continued*

Asset Disclosure Questionnaire		Yes	No	Details	Citation
Ministers / cabinet members					
37	Is public availability specified?				
38	Is the length of records maintenance specified?				
39	Are penalties for violating nondisclosure of declarations specified?				
Members of Parliament					
40	Is public availability specified?				
41	Is the length of records maintenance specified?				
42	Are penalties for violating nondisclosure of declarations specified?				
Civil servants					
43	Is public availability specified?				
44	Is the length of records maintenance specified?				
45	Are penalties for violating nondisclosure of declarations specified?				
Spouses and children					
46	Is public availability specified?				
47	Is the length of records maintenance specified?				
48	Are penalties for violating nondisclosure of declarations specified?				

TABLE A.10

Freedom of Information Questionnaire

Freedom of information questionnaire		Yes	No	Details	Citation
Legal framework					
1	Is there a legal right to access information?				
2	Is it a constitutional requirement?				
3	Is there a legislation governing access to information?				
4	Is there a right to appeal?				
Does access to information cover the following (check all that apply)?					
5	Drafts of legal instruments				
6	Enacted legal instruments				
7	Annual budgets				
8	Annual chart of accounts				
9	Annual reports				
What are the procedures for accessing information (check all that apply)?					
10	Written guidelines for request of information				
11	Written requests				
12	Electronic requests				
13	Oral requests				

(continued on next page)

TABLE A.10

Freedom of Information Questionnaire *Continued*

Freedom of information questionnaire		Yes	No	Details	Citation
Do the following exemptions to disclosure requirements apply?					
14	Exemptions to coverage				
15	Public Interest test				
16	Harm test				
Existence of appeals mechanism					
17	Are there appeals within public entities?				
18	Is there an independent nonjudicial appeals mechanism?				
19	Is there a judicial appeals mechanism?				
Enforcement mechanism					
20	Are there freedom of information act contact points?				
21	Is there a freedom of information act enforcement body?				
Do the following deadlines apply for release of information (check all that apply)?					
22	Initial response deadline of no more than 15 days				
23	Right to extend response time				
24	Maximum total response time of no more than 40 days				
25	Are nominal fees mandated?				
Sanctions for failure to disclose					
26	Are there administrative sanctions?				
27	Are there fines?				

APPENDIX B

Dynamics of Change: A Literature Review

Role of Transparency and Political Engagement in Improving Government Functioning

Political constraints often make it difficult to pursue policies that are technically sound. For example, governments often find it challenging to reduce subsides for various goods and services even when rigorous analysis shows that the benefits of such subsidies are not reaching the intended beneficiaries, such as poor people. A common reaction to such situations, including on the part of donors, is to accept the political constraints as given and look for second-based solutions that may be feasible in the given political scenario.

A recent World Bank study suggests more optimistic possibilities (World Bank 2016). On the basis of a rich survey of available literature, the report analyzes the political behavior of citizens, public officials, and leaders, and concludes that an appropriate mix of political mobilization and transparency measures can bring about significant change even in a challenging political economy. In other words, political constraints need not be taken as exogenous and that the constraints may be relaxed endogenously. However, this requires a good understanding of what incentives drive political behavior and in what manner.

World Bank (2016) highlights the role of citizens in the political process, particularly in selecting elected officials and in holding them accountable for delivery. Citizens may also run for office themselves. Political engagement by citizens creates pressure on the elected officials who, in turn, exercise their authority, whether as members of parliament or as ministers, to create pressure on the public institutions responsible for delivery.

The effectiveness of the political engagement of citizens, and perhaps its degree as well, is influenced by transparency measures. The report cites numerous studies that show how such measures, combined with political engagement, improve the performance of government. Nongovernmental actors, such as media, civil society organizations, nongovernmental organizations, think tanks, and business associations may generate and publicize data on various aspects of a government's work. They may organize events at which government officials, both politicians and bureaucrats, can have constructive discussion with stakeholders to understand the data better and agree on corrective actions. The government may also directly contribute to transparency through its disclosure policies. Technological developments are making it easier to both generate data as well as publicize them widely. Other developments, such as the spread of right to information legislation, are also helping.[1] Nonetheless, there are challenges and the report discusses both effective as well as ineffective attempts at enhancing transparency or using transparency as a driver for change.

The findings of World Bank (2016) have important implications for the work of external catalysts, including that done by the World Bank. The report states: "A lesson for us at the World Bank also comes out of this research. We can do more, through relatively small changes in what we are already doing, to leverage our technical strengths in generating credible data and evidence, and to work with our clients to diminish political constraints to achieving development goals" (World Bank 2016, x).

This study on privilege-resistant policy making is inspired by such a line of argument. It contributes to transparency in at least two ways. First, by benchmarking countries on dimensions of policy making that have implications for privilege seeking, it helps reveal how countries have made their policy regimes vulnerable to capture. The country-specific data, as well as cross-country comparisons, may thus help focus public attention on such deficiencies and generate pressure for change. Second, many of the policy features covered by this study are transparency-related, be it a database on investment incentives, online provision of information on documents and fees required to register a business, or publication of draft laws and regulations so that stakeholders may provide feedback.

World Bank (2016) argues that transparency initiatives should not focus on the mere provision of information but also pay attention to the specifics of the information shared, the manner in which it is made available and the purpose behind it. There is a caution: making governments more transparent is a challenge since the same political economy factors that make transparency important may also make it difficult to achieve.

Political engagement by citizens is likely to be most effective in democratic environments characterized by regular elections. This raises an important question about the scope for the political engagement of citizens, in combination with transparency measures, to make the needle move in the Middle East and North Africa context. However, World Bank (2016, 7) reassures us that "political engagement happens in every institutional context, from democracies to autocracies, albeit in different ways."[2] Although the process would differ, there are ways in which citizens may engage politically, armed with information, to help improve public sector delivery even in less democratic contexts.

Virtuous Cycles of Change and "Working with the Grain"

A recent publication (Levy 2014) provides another set of arguments and evidence on the possibilities of change even in situations with challenging political economy and governance characteristics. Partly based on direct experience gained through many years of governance work in the World Bank, Brian Levy states the case for "working with the grain" as a practical approach to finding islands of opportunity and triggering virtuous cycles of change. A few core ideas presented in this work are particularly relevant for our study.

First is the concept of "islands of effectiveness"—pockets of good governance, sound policy making and effective implementation—amid a sea of governance dysfunction. These islands are often created and sustained by horizontal, peer-to-peer stakeholder interactions in government agencies, which may be distinguished from top-down attempts to resolve principal-agent problems in government that usually require strong, sustained leadership. Horizontal reform efforts in the pursuit of islands of effectiveness may be pursued even in the absence of such leadership.

The second idea is that of virtuous cycles of change which, in Levy's analysis (2014), is driven by three mutually reinforcing factors: inclusive growth, positive expectations, and ongoing institutional performance. Positive changes in any of these drivers may induce similar changes in the others, with the feedback loop often completed as the second-round changes further improve performance on the initial driver. For example, sustained growth, especially if it is inclusive, may strengthen the private sector, civil society, and the middle class population, which, in turn, demand better performance from public sector institutions, including through policy and regulatory reforms. These demands are often the result of positive expectations generated by growth. For example, sustained growth may create expectations of high returns on investment, but these additional investments may require a conducive business environment. The expectations of high returns may create additional incentive for businesses to lobby ever more strongly for business environment reforms. Growth, by expanding the fiscal space for governments, may also help build the capacity required in government agencies to bring about the changes demanded by stakeholders. Levy argues, "With continued forward momentum, institutions can strengthen incrementally, gradually transforming personalized into more impersonal arrangement."

Levy's articulation of a model of virtuous cycle of change follows the tradition of scholars such as Albert Hirschman and Douglass North who argued that development is an ongoing, cumulative process where small, individual changes, by reinforcing each other, can lead to transformative change. The reinforcement comes from the interconnectedness of the small initiatives. Initiators of a small change may believe that its impact will be modest. Such actors, whether in government or outside, are usually unable to comprehend even partly, leave alone fully, the ripple effect of their actions. However, for a variety of reasons, they are motivated to take that small initiative. How does one identify such actors, understand their motivations and help create conditions that may trigger such initiatives, thus converting motivations into actual actions? And, having helped to trigger the initial change, how can one create conditions for the ripple effects to play out so that a cumulative change process is unleashed? These questions bring us to the third important idea of the book, which is reflected in its title, that is, "working with the grain" and summarized by Levy: "Effective action will seek to work with rather than against a country's grain in order to nudge forward this interdependent, dynamic process."

The "working with the grain" approach moves away from a formulaic, best-practice way of fostering change to one that recognizes that there can be multiple pathways to initiating and sustaining change and that the choice of a path should be well grounded in the institutional and political economy reality of a country. This approach recognizes path-dependence and the importance of understanding the trajectory that a country, government or society is on, where it is currently placed on that trajectory and where it can feasibly move to. These trajectories define both needs and possibilities, and working with the grain implies identifying and supporting reforms that correspond to these. It is a good-fit approach rather than a best-practice approach. It involves finding the right entry point that creates, or strengthens, islands of effectiveness and unleashes a virtuous cycle of change.

Mind, Behavior, and Nudging

The World Bank 2015 *World Development Report* examines the role of human behavior and incentives in decision making, including decisions that relate to the subject matter of this study, such as the award of privileges to well-connected businesses or initiating reforms to restrain such actions. Human behavior is influenced by psychological, social, and cultural factors and this, in turn, shapes the decisions and actions people take, including the decision not to act. What may appear as irrational behavior is, according to this approach, often a perfectly rational behavior following from the particular objective functions of the decision makers and the constraints in which they operate. The 2015 *World Development Report* summarizes research findings that show how such change agents may harness such influences on people's behavior, instead of taking them as given, to induce desirable decisions and initiatives. The wealth of evidence in the report relates to a diverse range of challenges, such as inducing households to save more, firms to increase productivity, and consumers to save energy.

A core message of the *World Development Report* (2015) is the need to identify not only what type of change to bring but also how. The report emphasizes the importance of understanding what motivates people to initiate change, and what inspires others to learn from pioneers and replicate such changes. It also underscores the need to experiment, adapt, and learn as implementation proceeds. It recognizes that people have psychological biases that affect decision making. Thus, a good understanding of such biases not only helps prevent interventions that are doomed to failure because they go against the biases but also, on a more positive note, helps leverage some biases to catalyze desirable change. This line of thinking leads to the concept of the nudge, whereby actors, such as government officials, are steered toward actions aligned with their intrinsic motivations and yet lead to desirable outcomes (Sunstein and Thaler 2008). This is different from a prescriptive command and control approach that is often difficult to implement given people's psychological biases. The nudge approach is increasingly being used to catalyze reforms in government, an example being the work of the Behavioral Insights Team in the U.K. government.

Notes

1. According to the report, 99 countries have enacted right-to-information legislation as of 2014, compared with only 29 countries that had done so by 2000.
2. It further states that "Even when formal institutions restrict the power of "ordinary" citizens, who hold no public office and are not organized into influential groups, research suggests that leaders are nevertheless constrained by the informal powers of nonelite citizens to engage in protests or revolts" (56).

References

Levy, Brian. 2014. *Working with the Grain: Integrating Governance and Growth in Development Strategy*. Oxford, UK: Oxford University Press.

Sunstein, Cass, and Richard Thaler. 2008. *Nudge: Improving Decisions about Health, Wealth, and Happiness*. New York: Penguin Books.

World Bank. 2015. *World Development Report: Mind, Society, and Behavior*. Washington, DC: World Bank.

———. 2016. *Making Politics Work for Development: Harnessing Transparency and Citizen Engagement*. Washington, DC: World Bank.

APPENDIX C

Stimulating Change for Privilege-Resistant Policy Making

The strands of work summarized in appendix B share some common ideas. Change is possible even in seemingly intractable situations. Potentially far-reaching change processes may be unleashed even through small changes in one part of the system. Even in a scenario of widespread dysfunction, there may exist "islands of opportunities" through which the small, initial changes may be carried out. A change in one part of a system may generate ripple effects as others observe the changes and are motivated to introduce similar changes in their jurisdictions. Sometimes, these second-order changes may directly build upon or complement the first-order changes; sometimes these may happen in parallel with no obvious synergy. Over time, however, synergy may develop between a set of such parallel changes, thus triggering a cumulative process of transformative change. This reasoning is the essence of Levy's "working with the grain" approach, articulated in Levy (2014), and it follows from the vast literature summarized in World Bank (2016) on political engagement by citizens and its synergy with transparency, and the *World Development Report* 2015's work on mind, society, and behavior.

The strands of work summarized in appendix B see possibilities in the behavioral tendencies of people, even if at first glance these appear irrational or immune to change. Interventions such as political engagement of citizens and transparency-enhancing actions leverage human incentives: they work with the grain of human behavior, often through small nudges, instead of attempting big changes that are contextually inappropriate.

Drawing from the aforementioned insights, we develop a model of change related to the agenda underlying this study, that is, how to initiate reforms that may make policy systems privilege resistant, especially in countries with a challenging political economy and governance context. This work is motivated by the belief that, in any country at a given point in time, a set of feasible actions exist that may enhance the privilege resistance of the government's policy apparatus, and that a sequence of such actions implemented over time may have a cumulative effect, often by setting in motion a virtuous cycle of change. Thus, even though the problem of privilege-driven policy making may appear intractable in the absence of a revolutionary change in politics, such incremental actions could make a serious dent in the system. This argument is developed below through the articulation of a model of change.

There are two stages of the change process in our model: (a) the initiation of change (reforms) in one part of government, and (b) the ripple effect of the initial reform that results in a virtuous cycle of change. We suggest that there are two main drivers of change in each of these stages: (a) a desire to do good on the part of some government functionaries; and (b) transparency enhancing measures. The former is the ignition of change and the latter the fuel that keeps the engine running.

Bureaucratic Motivations: Desire to Do Good versus Playing It Safe

Our model has three actors: (a) the political leadership (such as ministers) that provides guidance and signals, sets the parameters within which policy is formulated, and approves the important policies; (b) the top bureaucrats who formulate the policies and have approval authority over some policies and rules; and (c) the mid level bureaucrats who implement policy and can enact good practice initiatives within the set policy parameters.

In this model, we assume that the political leadership and top bureaucrats determine the scope for privileged treatment through their policy-setting roles and the award of privileges through their administrative approval authority. The mid-level bureaucrats may indulge in petty corruption, exploiting their front-line implementation roles, but do not have an important role in the award of major privileges (we are making a distinction between major privileges and favors given by officials in return for small bribes; only the former is the subject of this study). However, mid-level officials may take initiatives that may constrain privilege seeking.

The core actor in our model is the mid-level bureaucrat, henceforth called the official.[1] In this model, officials are driven by two considerations: (a) having a quiet life versus (b) proactively doing some good. We suggest that government officials are often motivated to lead a quiet life of acquiescence in which they passively agree with the decisions of their superiors (such as the top policy makers) and colleagues even if they do not agree with them personally. At the same time, officials like to do something good such as making sure government actions, whether important policy decisions or small projects, serve broad societal interest rather than the interests of a privileged few. Such motivations may be triggered by factors such as patriotism, pride in one's job, or empathy with ordinary people.

In our model, there is a trade-off between these two motivations. A desire to do good will often mean sacrificing a quiet life. This trade-off is depicted in figure C.1. Curves I and II represent a set of indifference curves showing the trade-off between the motivations. When on a particular indifference curve, say curve I, officials are able to do more good (that is, move right along the horizontal axis) only if they are willing to sacrifice a quiet life (that is, move down the vertical axis), and vice versa. The slope of the indifference curve shows how large the trade-off is. However, there are costs to both. Acquiescing in wrong decisions now in order to lead a quiet life may incur costs, including a feeling of personal guilt as well as the possibility of disciplinary action later. On the other hand, doing some good may also have costs. For example, opposing the grant of privileges to a select few may mean going against the wishes of bosses and colleagues, thus disturbing collegiality, and may even incur the

FIGURE C.1

Bureaucratic Decision-Making Equilibrium

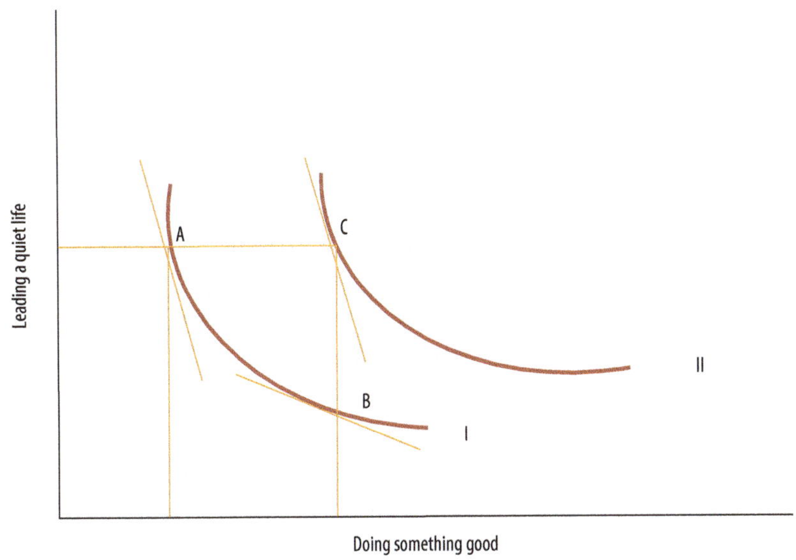

wrath of powerful people inside and outside government. It may lead to career stagnation and inconvenient postings, or even job losses and other more extreme forms of harassments. These relative costs are captured by the straight line touching the indifference curve I. Utility is maximized at point A; hence, this is the initial equilibrium. As we can see, in the particular scenario depicted by figure C.1, the officials like to play it safe and their proclivity to do good is rather limited.

In this model, government officials could be motivated to do more good in two ways. First, the relative costs of playing it safe compared to doing good may be changed. This will be represented by a change in the slope of the relative cost line. For example, a flattening of the line will generate a new equilibrium (at point B) in which officials are more willing to disturb the status quo so that they can do more good. Alternatively, if the indifference curve itself shifts to curve II, officials can do more good without sacrificing a quiet life (moving to point C) (figure C.1).

Initiation of Change

We shall now discuss some operational ways in which the above changes in figure C.1 (shifts in the indifference curve or changes in the slope of the cost line) can be triggered, thus creating the initial impetus for change. Let us consider the case of a database on investment incentives. A small group of government officials, or even an individual, can work quietly to pull together data on existing investment incentives, including names of awardees. Such a database may reveal privileged treatment and create pressure for corrective actions in future when a more conducive environment exists for such action. In the short run, such a surreptitious act of creating a database may not disturb the quiet life of the officials while allowing them the pleasure of doing something good. The opportunity to create such a database implies a shift in the indifference curve from I to II (and a move from A to B) in figure C.1.

Alternatively, let us assume there is a regime change in which some people in important government positions (perhaps a new minister, or an existing minister who develops an interest in reforms) decide to make the incentive regime less privilege-driven. This changes the relative cost line. With new signals coming from the top, the costs of doing something good (such as incurring the displeasure of bosses or colleagues) is now reduced. This is the same as a move from A to B (see figure C.1).

The appointment of a new minister who wants to make policy regimes privilege-resistant can be seen as a positive exogenous shock to the system. External change agents, such as donors, are sometimes able to catalyze such changes, but in our model we do not consider such options.

Thus, this change is truly exogenous. However, often a reform-minded minister is unclear about which actions to take within an agenda, or even which agenda to pick. The minister is simply interested in doing something good and important. An external change agent, such as a donor, or internal change agents, such as reform-minded government officials, can steer such a minister toward a specific privilege-resisting agenda, such as reforming an investment incentive regime. Such an engagement helps convert the minister's general desire to do something good to a concrete agenda for action.

However, having now focused on a specific agenda, the minister will need tools to get the agenda endorsed (for example, get support at the cabinet) and then implement it. Let us continue with the example of investment incentives. Let us assume that, thanks to a World Bank project and the actions of a small group of officials who wanted to do some good, a solid database on investment incentives was created and maintained for a few years before this minister took office. Also, an assessment of the impact of such incentives has been carried out that showed the limited impact, or complete ineffectiveness, of the incentive regime—not a surprising result given that incentives are driven by privileges, and not any efficiency consideration. The database and analysis was not used before because the conditions were not conducive.

Now these outputs and tools (the database and the economic analysis) are useful. They allow the minister to go to the cabinet or head of government and make a case for incentive reforms. The important thing is the availability of the tools. If these are not readily available, some time would have to be spent in creating the database and carrying out the assessment. Such scenarios are common, and World Bank projects often support such work after a reform champion has emerged and asks for ideas. The project outputs help design the reforms. However, often the window of opportunity is limited, and by the time an output is produced, conditions may change—either the reform champion is gone or has changed his or her mind. Thus, it is often helpful to have such work done ahead of time so the tools are ready when a reform champion emerges. Often, mid-level bureaucrats can carry out such work surreptitiously and wait for a propitious moment to use it. Even in the short run, that is, before that big moment arrives, such initiatives may make some dent in the system towards greater privilege resistance.

Even in a privilege-driven atmosphere, there is scope for the World Bank and other external catalysts to support initiatives that bring modest, but potentially powerful, changes in the system, while generating tools that are useful in more propitious circumstances. These initiatives are compatible with the incentives of the officials and illustrate the principle of "working with the grain."

From One Change to More

The role of transparency and other disciplining measures in strengthening the impetus of change is further explained by the three corrective or preventive mechanisms discussed in chapter 2: (a) conflict of interest restrictions, (b) financial disclosure, and (c) freedom of information. Here we relate these important areas to our behavioral model. As explained in chapter 2, conflict of interest restrictions provide clear definitions of prohibited conduct. This affects top officials, who are the main grantors of privileges in our model, as well as their subordinates (the mid-level bureaucrats) who do not grant privileges but can oppose such actions by their superiors. First, such restrictions reduce the degree of impunity felt by the top officials and may thus change their calculations of the costs and benefits of granting privileges to cronies. Mid-level officials may refer to such restrictions when they refuse to acquiesce to the grant of privileges by their superiors.

In our model, this has two effects. First, superiors are less likely to put pressure on subordinates to acquiesce in the granting of privileges, since the costs of potential whistle-blowing is greater. This enlarges the space for mid-level officials to do some good. Thus, the indifference curve shifts to the right. Second, the costs of acquiescing becomes greater because mid-level officials may also be subject to greater scrutiny. These effects change the costs of leading a quiet life (which has now gone up) relative to that of doing some good. This leads to a flatter relative cost curve. Both effects are in the same direction and combine to move the equilibrium toward a more desirable direction, that is, from A to C (in figure C.2). Mid-level officials are now able to do greater good (as shown by the horizontal arrow in figure C.2) while willing to sacrifice a bit of their quiet life (vertical arrow). As discussed in chapter 2, the effect of conflict of interest restrictions is further enhanced if there are requirements for financial disclosure and provisions for freedom of information.

Virtuous Cycle of Change

The second dimension of our model is about how an initial reform action can eventually trigger a virtuous cycle of change through a series of ripple effects. A reform action in one area can demonstrate the benefits of reform to stakeholders within the government, both functionaries in the agency carrying out the reform, and in other parts of government. It may also show to risk-averse bureaucrats that actual

FIGURE C.2

Triggering Change in Bureaucratic Decisions

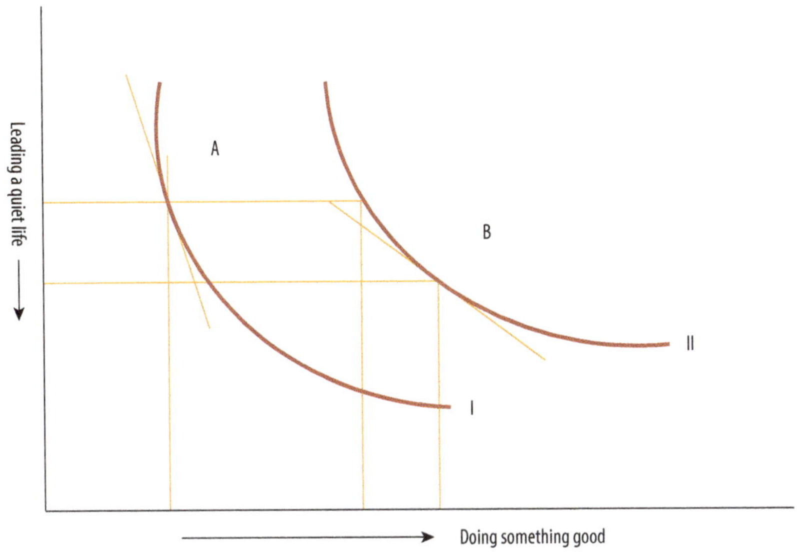

risks of carrying out a reform are less than perceived, thus reducing their resistance to change.

The ripple effect of an initial reform may follow different paths. Figure C.3 illustrates this using the policy areas and policy governance dimensions covered by this study. Let us assume that, through dynamics similar to those described in the previous section, a reform champion takes action to introduce rule-based decision making in the allocation of public land. This is shown as the "first-round reform" in figure C.3. Once that reform has taken hold and its benefits demonstrated, the same reform champion or others involved in the allocation of public land decide to consolidate the gains through additional reforms. Thus, they may establish a grievance mechanism to address cases in which applicants for public land feel that the rule-based decision-making process has not worked well for them. They may also want to put their initial reform (establishment of rule-based decision making) on a more solid footing by creating an appropriate policy and legal framework for it.[2]

Once the reform momentum gets further consolidated, a third round of reforms may be initiated. Thus, the authorities in charge of land allocation may now be ready to become even more participatory and transparent by putting in place mechanisms for stakeholder consultation and public sharing of information on allocation of public land. This third round of reforms often requires an even greater amount of courage since these imply opening up to scrutiny by a broad range of stakeholders

FIGURE C.3

Ripple Effects of Initial Reforms

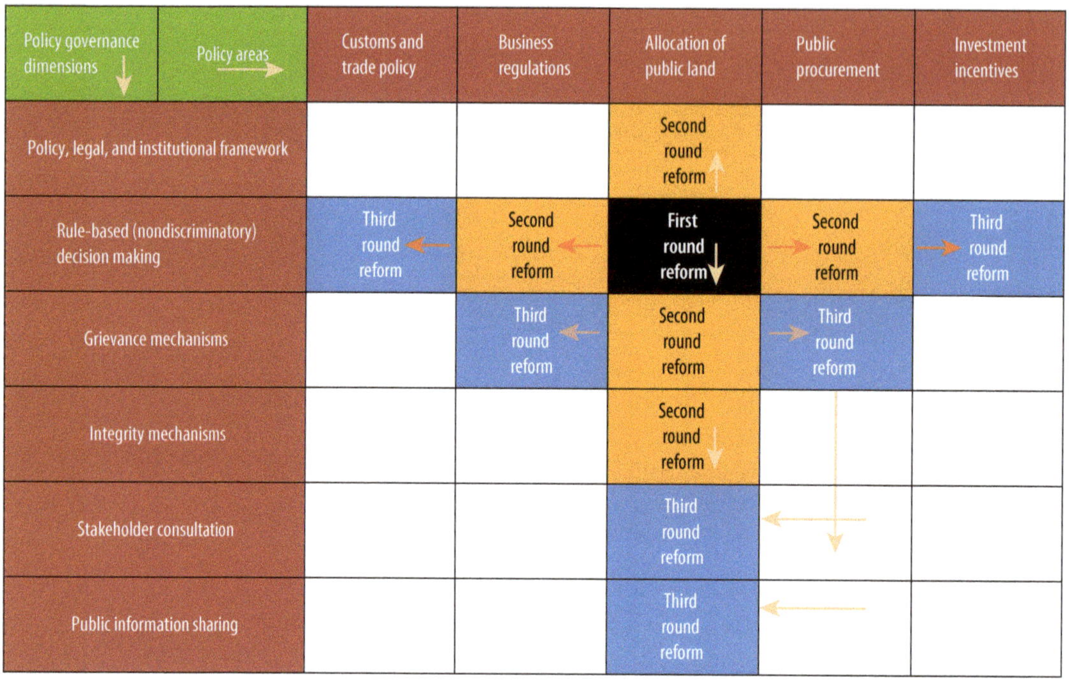

outside the government. Thus, government officials may initially be willing to interact with nongovernmental stakeholders on a limited basis, such as through a grievance mechanism, but not in a more open manner. However, after testing results of a limited grievance mechanism, they may muster the courage to go for more participatory and transparent systems.

The aforementioned scenario exemplifies what may be called a vertical set of "reform ripple" effects in which the second and third rounds of reforms happen in the same policy area as the initial reform (shown by the yellow arrows in figure C.3). Another scenario is that of a horizontal set of ripple effects as shown by the orange arrows. Here, the establishment of a system of rule-based decision making in the allocation of public land triggers the establishment of similar systems in other policy areas. For example, as depicted in figure C.3, rule-based decision making is now introduced in the area of public procurement and business regulations. This is the second round of reforms. Subsequently, there is a third round in which similar systems are introduced for customs and trade, and for investment incentives.

We can add further nuances to this model and consider scenarios that combine horizontal and vertical movements. For example, the establishment of rule-based decision making in the allocation of public land may lead to a vertical ripple effect by encouraging the land authority to establish grievance mechanisms as well. However, the vertical effects do not go any further than this, and no further reforms happen in land allocation (at least not for a while). Instead, in the third round, grievance mechanisms are triggered in other policy areas, such as public procurement and business regulation (as shown by the peach arrow). In this way, reforms in one policy area trigger reforms in other areas.

Eventually, these ripple effects may find their way back to the initial reform arena. Thus, the transparency initiatives in the area of public land allocation (grievance mechanisms) may be taken further with the establishment of stakeholder consultation mechanisms and public sharing of information in the same policy area. This may then encourage other parts of government, such as responsible for land allocation, to open up (dotted lines in figure C.3). As we discussed in chapters 1 and 2, such transparency measures may create pressure to sustain and strengthen the initial reform in land allocation, that is, the introduction of rule-based decision making. When that happens, the rounds of ripple effects bring the story full circle; that is, a virtuous cycle of reforms is established.

Notes

1. Although the mid-level bureaucrat is the core actor in this model, the role and incentives attributed to the mid-level official may also apply to some senior officials.
2. In a classic scenario, the policy and legal framework may come first, followed by the specific processes or systems that the framework is supposed to underpin. However, in the real world, reforms sometimes follow an idiosyncratic, opportunistic path and are initiated in the middle, rather the beginning, of a stylized linear sequence.

References

Levy, Brian. 2014. *Working with the Grain: Integrating Governance and Growth in Development Strategy*. Oxford, U.K.: Oxford University Press.

World Bank. 2016. "Making Politics Work for Development: Harnessing Transparency and Citizen Engagement." Policy Research Report, World Bank, Washington, DC.

ECO-AUDIT

Environmental Benefits Statement

The World Bank Group is committed to reducing its environmental footprint. In support of this commitment, we leverage electronic publishing options and print-on-demand technology, which is located in regional hubs worldwide. Together, these initiatives enable print runs to be lowered and shipping distances decreased, resulting in reduced paper consumption, chemical use, greenhouse gas emissions, and waste.

We follow the recommended standards for paper use set by the Green Press Initiative. The majority of our books are printed on Forest Stewardship Council (FSC)–certified paper, with nearly all containing 50–100 percent recycled content. The recycled fiber in our book paper is either unbleached or bleached using totally chlorine-free (TCF), processed chlorine–free (PCF), or enhanced elemental chlorine–free (EECF) processes.

More information about the Bank's environmental philosophy can be found at http://www.worldbank.org/corporateresponsibility.

green press INITIATIVE

www.ingramcontent.com/pod-product-compliance
Ingram Content Group UK Ltd.
Pitfield, Milton Keynes, MK11 3LW, UK
UKHW050426250626
472619UK00007B/250

9 781464 812071